Print vs. Digital:
The Future of Coexistence

Print vs. Digital: The Future of Coexistence has been co-published simultaneously as *Journal of Library Administration*, Volume 46, Number 2 2007.

Monographs from the *Journal of Library Administration*®

For additional information on these and other Haworth Press titles, including descriptions, tables of contents, reviews, and prices, use the QuickSearch catalog at http://www.HaworthPress.com.

1. *Planning for Library Services: A Guide to Utilizing Planning Methods for Library Management,* edited by Charles R. McClure, PhD (Vol. 2, No. 3/4, 1982). *"Should be read by anyone who is involved in planning processes of libraries–certainly by every administrator of a library or system." (American Reference Books Annual)*

2. *Finance Planning for Libraries,* edited by Murray S. Martin (Vol. 3, No. 3/4, 1983). *Stresses the need for libraries to weed out expenditures which do not contribute to their basic role–the collection and organization of information–when planning where and when to spend money.*

3. *Marketing and the Library,* edited by Gary T. Ford (Vol. 4, No. 4, 1984). *Discover the latest methods for more effective information dissemination and learn to develop successful programs for specific target areas.*

4. *Excellence in Library Management,* edited by Charlotte Georgi, MLS, and Robert Bellanti, MLS, MBA (Vol. 6, No. 3, 1985). *"Most beneficial for library administrators . . . for anyone interested in either library/information science or management." (Special Libraries)*

5. *Archives and Library Administration: Divergent Traditions and Common Concerns,* edited by Lawrence J. McCrank, PhD, MLS (Vol. 7, No. 2/3, 1986). *"A forward-looking view of archives and libraries. . . . Recommend[ed] to students, teachers, and practitioners alike of archival and library science. It is readable, thought-provoking, and provides a summary of the major areas of divergence and convergence." (Association of Canadian Map Libraries and Archives)*

6. *Legal Issues for Library and Information Managers,* edited by William Z. Nasri, JD, PhD (Vol. 7, No. 4, 1986). *"Useful to any librarian looking for protection or wondering where responsibilities end and liabilities begin. Recommended." (Academic Library Book Review)*

7. *Pricing and Costs of Monographs and Serials: National and International Issues,* edited by Sul H. Lee (Supp. #l, 1987). *"Eminently readable. There is a good balance of chapters on serials and monographs and the perspective of suppliers, publishers, and library practitioners are presented. A book well worth reading." (Australasian College Libraries)*

8. *Management Issues in the Networking Environment,* edited by Edward R. Johnson, PhD (Vol. 8, No. 3/4, 1987). *"Particularly useful for librarians/information specialists contemplating establishing a local network." (Australian Library Review)*

9. *Library Management and Technical Services: The Changing Role of Technical Services in Library Organizations,* edited by Jennifer Cargill, MSLS, MSEd (Vol. 9, No. 1, 1988). *"As a practical and instructive guide to issues such as automation, personnel matters, education, management techniques and liaison with other services, senior library managers with a sincere interest in evaluating the role of their technical services should find this a timely publication." (Library Association Record)*

10. *Computing, Electronic Publishing, and Information Technology: Their Impact on Academic Libraries,* edited by Robin N. Downes (Vol. 9, No. 4, 1988). *"For a relatively short and easily digestible discussion of these issues, this book can be recommended, not only to those in academic libraries, but also to those in similar types of library or information unit, and to academics and educators in the field." (Journal of Documentation)*

11. *Acquisitions, Budgets, and Material Costs: Issues and Approaches,* edited by Sul H. Lee (Supp. #2, 1988). *"The advice of these library practitioners is sensible and their insights illuminating for librarians in academic libraries." (American Reference Books Annual)*

12. *The Impact of Rising Costs of Serials and Monographs on Library Services and Programs,* edited by Sul H. Lee (Vol. 10, No. 1, 1989). *". . . Sul Lee hit a winner here." (Serials Review)*

13. *Creativity, Innovation, and Entrepreneurship in Libraries,* edited by Donald E. Riggs, EdD, MLS (Vol. 10, No. 2/3, 1989). *"The volume is well worth reading as a whole. . . . There is very little repetition, and it should stimulate thought." (Australian Library Review)*

14. *Human Resources Management in Libraries,* edited by Gisela M. Webb, MLS, MPA (Vol. 10, No. 4, 1989). *"Thought provoking and enjoyable reading. . . . Provides valuable insights for the effective information manager." (Special Libraries)*

15. *Managing Public Libraries in the 21st Century,* edited by Pat Woodrum, MLS (Vol. 11, No. 1/2, 1989). *"A broad-based collection of topics that explores the management problems and possibilities public libraries will be facing in the 21st century." (Robert Swisher, PhD, Director, School of Library and Information Studies, University of Oklahoma)*

16. *Library Education and Employer Expectations,* edited by E. Dale Cluff, PhD, MLS (Vol. 11, No. 3/4, 1990). *"Useful to library-school students and faculty interested in employment problems and employer perspectives. Librarians concerned with recruitment practices will also be interested." (Information Technology and Libraries)*

17. *Training Issues and Strategies in Libraries,* edited by Paul M. Gherman, MALS, and Frances O. Painter, MLS, MBA (Vol. 12, No. 2, 1990). *"There are . . . useful chapters, all by different authors, each with a preliminary summary of the content–a device that saves much time in deciding whether to read the whole chapter or merely skim through it. Many of the chapters are essentially practical without too much emphasis on theory. This book is a good investment." (Library Association Record)*

18. *Library Material Costs and Access to Information,* edited by Sul H. Lee (Vol. 12, No. 3, 1990). *"A cohesive treatment of the issue. Although the book's contributors possess a research library perspective, the data and the ideas presented are of interest and benefit to the entire profession, especially academic librarians." (Library Resources and Technical Services)*

19. *Library Development: A Future Imperative,* edited by Dwight F. Burlingame, PhD (Vol. 12, No. 4, 1990). *"This volume provides an excellent overview of fundraising with special application to libraries. . . . A useful book that is highly recommended for all libraries." (Library Journal)*

20. *Personnel Administration in an Automated Environment,* edited by Philip E. Leinbach, MLS (Vol. 13, No. 1/2, 1990). *"An interesting and worthwhile volume, recommended to university library administrators and to others interested in thought-provoking discussion of the personnel implications of automation." (Canadian Library Journal)*

21. *Strategic Planning in Higher Education: Implementing New Roles for the Academic Library,* edited by James F. Williams, II, MLS (Vol. 13, No. 3/4, 1991). *"A welcome addition to the sparse literature on strategic planning in university libraries. Academic librarians considering strategic planning for their libraries will learn a great deal from this work." (Canadian Library Journal)*

22. *Creative Planning for Library Administration: Leadership for the Future,* edited by Kent Hendrickson, MALS (Vol. 14, No. 2, 1991). *"Provides some essential information on the planning process, and the mix of opinions and methodologies, as well as examples relevant to every library manager, resulting in a very readable foray into a topic too long avoided by many of us." (Canadian Library Journal)*

23. *Budgets for Acquisitions: Strategies for Serials, Monographs, and Electronic Formats,* edited by Sul H. Lee (Vol. 14, No. 3, 1991). *"Much more than a series of handy tips for the careful shopper. This [book] is a most useful one–well-informed, thought-provoking, and authoritative." (Australian Library Review)*

24. *Managing Technical Services in the 90's,* edited by Drew Racine (Vol. 15, No. 1/2, 1991). *"Presents an eclectic overview of the challenges currently facing all library technical services efforts. . . . Recommended to library administrators and interested practitioners." (Library Journal)*

25. *Library Management in the Information Technology Environment: Issues, Policies, and Practice for Administrators,* edited by Brice G. Hobrock, PhD, MLS (Vol. 15, No. 3/4, 1992). *"A road map to identify some of the alternative routes to the electronic library." (Stephen Rollins, Associate Dean for Library Services, General Library, University of New Mexico)*

26. *The Management of Library and Information Studies Education,* edited by Herman L. Totten, PhD, MLS (Vol. 16, No. 1/2, 1992). *"Offers something of interest to everyone connected with LIS education–the undergraduate contemplating a master's degree, the doctoral student struggling with courses and career choices, the new faculty member aghast at conflicting responsibilities, the experienced but stressed LIS professor, and directors of LIS Schools." (Education Libraries)*

27. *Vendor Evaluation and Acquisition Budgets,* edited by Sul H. Lee (Vol. 16, No. 3, 1992). *"The title doesn't do justice to the true scope of this excellent collection of papers delivered at the sixth annual conference on library acquisitions sponsored by the University of Oklahoma Libraries." (Kent K. Hendrickson, BS, MALS, Dean of Libraries, University of Nebraska-Lincoln) Find insightful discussions on the impact of rising costs on library budgets and management in this groundbreaking book.*

28. *Developing Library Staff for the 21st Century,* edited by Maureen Sullivan (Vol. 17, No. 1, 1992). *"I found myself enthralled with this highly readable publication. It is one of those rare compilations that manages to successfully integrate current general management operational thinking in the context of academic library management." (Bimonthly Review of Law Books)*

29. *Collection Assessment and Acquisitions Budgets,* edited by Sul H. Lee (Vol. 17, No. 2, 1993). *Contains timely information about the assessment of academic library collections and the relationship of collection assessment to acquisition budgets.*

30. *Leadership in Academic Libraries: Proceedings of the W. Porter Kellam Conference, The University of Georgia, May 7, 1991,* edited by William Gray Potter (Vol. 17, No. 4, 1993). *"Will be of interest to those concerned with the history of American academic libraries." (Australian Library Review)*

31. *Integrating Total Quality Management in a Library Setting,* edited by Susan Jurow, MLS, and Susan B. Barnard, MLS (Vol. 18, No. 1/2, 1993). *"Especially valuable are the librarian experiences that directly relate to real concerns about TQM. Recommended for all professional reading collections." (Library Journal)*

32. *Catalysts for Change: Managing Libraries in the 1990s,* edited by Gisela M. von Dran, DPA, MLS, and Jennifer Cargill, MSLS, MSEd (Vol. 18, No. 3/4, 1993). *"A useful collection of articles which focuses on the need for librarians to employ enlightened management practices in order to adapt to and thrive in the rapidly changing information environment." (Australian Library Review)*

33. *The Role and Future of Special Collections in Research Libraries: British and American Perspectives,* edited by Sul H. Lee (Vol. 19, No. 1, 1993). *"A provocative but informative read for library users, academic administrators, and private sponsors." (International Journal of Information and Library Research)*

34. *Declining Acquisitions Budgets: Allocation, Collection Development and Impact Communication,* edited by Sul H. Lee (Vol. 19, No. 2, 1993). *"Expert and provocative. . . . Presents many ways of looking at library budget deterioration and responses to it . . . There is much food for thought here." (Library Resources & Technical Services)*

35. *Libraries as User-Centered Organizations: Imperatives for Organizational Change,* edited by Meredith A. Butler (Vol. 19, No. 3/4, 1993). *"Presents a very timely and well-organized discussion of major trends and influences causing organizational changes." (Science Books & Films)*

36. *Access, Ownership, and Resource Sharing,* edited by Sul H. Lee (Vol. 20, No. 1, 1994). *The contributing authors present a useful and informative look at the current status of information provision and some of the challenges the subject presents.*

37. *The Dynamic Library Organizations in a Changing Environment,* edited by Joan Giesecke, MLS, DPA (Vol. 20, No. 2, 1994). *"Provides a significant look at potential changes in the library world and presents its readers with possible ways to address the negative results of such changes. . . . Covers the key issues facing today's libraries . . . Two thumbs up!" (Marketing Library Resources)*

38. **The Future of Information Services,** edited by Virginia Steel, MA, and C. Brigid Welch, MLS (Vol. 20, No. 3/4, 1995). *"The leadership discussions will be useful for library managers as will the discussions of how library structures and services might work in the next century." (Australian Special Libraries)*

39. **The Future of Resource Sharing,** edited by Shirley K. Baker and Mary E. Jackson, MLS (Vol. 21, No. 1/2, 1995). *"Recommended for library and information science schools because of its balanced presentation of the ILL/document delivery issues." (Library Acquisitions: Practice and Theory)*

40. **Libraries and Student Assistants: Critical Links,** edited by William K. Black, MLS (Vol. 21, No. 3/4, 1995). *"A handy reference work on many important aspects of managing student assistants. . . . Solid, useful information on basic management issues in this work and several chapters are useful for experienced managers." (The Journal of Academic Librarianship)*

41. **Managing Change in Academic Libraries,** edited by Joseph J. Branin (Vol. 22, No. 2/3, 1996). *"Touches on several aspects of academic library management, emphasizing the changes that are occurring at the present time. . . . Recommended this title for individuals or libraries interested in management aspects of academic libraries." (RQ American Library Association)*

42. **Access, Resource Sharing and Collection Development,** edited by Sul H. Lee (Vol. 22, No. 4, 1996). *Features continuing investigation and discussion of important library issues, specifically the role of libraries in acquiring, storing, and disseminating information in different formats.*

43. **Interlibrary Loan/Document Delivery and Customer Satisfaction: Strategies for Redesigning Services,** edited by Pat L. Weaver-Meyers, Wilbur A. Stolt, and Yem S. Fong (Vol. 23, No. 1/2, 1997). *"No interlibrary loan department supervisor at any mid-sized to large college or university library can afford not to read this book." (Gregg Sapp, MLS, MEd, Head of Access Services, University of Miami, Richter Library, Coral Gables, Florida)*

44. **Emerging Patterns of Collection Development in Expanding Resource Sharing, Electronic Information, and Network Environment,** edited by Sul H. Lee (Vol. 24, No. 1/2, 1997). *"The issues it deals with are common to us all. We all need to make our funds go further and our resources work harder, and there are ideas here which we can all develop." (The Library Association Record)*

45. **The Academic Library Director: Reflections on a Position in Transition,** edited by Frank D'Andraia, MLS (Vol. 24, No. 3, 1997). *"A useful collection to have whether you are seeking a position as director or conducting a search for one." (College & Research Libraries News)*

46. **Economics of Digital Information: Collection, Storage, and Delivery,** edited by Sul H. Lee (Vol. 24, No. 4, 1997). *Highlights key concepts and issues vital to a library's successful venture into the digital environment and helps you understand why the transition from the printed page to the digital packet has been problematic for both creators of proprietary materials and users of those materials.*

47. **Management of Library and Archival Security: From the Outside Looking In,** edited by Robert K. O'Neill, PhD (Vol. 25, No. 1, 1998). *"Provides useful advice and on-target insights for professionals caring for valuable documents and artifacts." (Menzi L. Behrnd-Klodt, JD, Attorney/Archivist, Klodt and Associates, Madison, WI)*

48. **OCLC 1967-1997: Thirty Years of Furthering Access to the World's Information,** edited by K. Wayne Smith (Vol. 25, No. 2/3/4, 1998). *"A rich–and poignantly personal, at times–historical account of what is surely one of this century's most important developments in librarianship." (Deanna B. Marcum, PhD, President, Council on Library and Information Resources, Washington, DC)*

49. **The Economics of Information in the Networked Environment,** edited by Meredith A. Butler, MLS, and Bruce R. Kingma, PhD (Vol. 26, No. 1/2, 1998). *"A book that should be read both by information professionals and by administrators, faculty and others who share a collective concern to provide the most information to the greatest number at the lowest cost in the networked environment." (Thomas J. Galvin, PhD, Professor of Information Science and Policy, University at Albany, State University of New York)*

50. *Information Technology Planning,* edited by Lori A. Goetsch (Vol. 26, No. 3/4, 1999). *Offers innovative approaches and strategies useful in your library and provides some food for thought about information technology as we approach the millennium.*

51. *Managing Multicultural Diversity in the Library: Principles and Issues for Administrators,* edited by Mark Winston (Vol. 27, No. 1/2, 1999). *Defines diversity, clarifies why it is important to address issues of diversity, and identifies goals related to diversity and how to go about achieving those goals.*

52. *Scholarship, Research Libraries, and Global Publishing,* by Jutta Reed-Scott (Vol. 27, No. 3/4, 1999). *This book documents a research project in conjunction with the Association of Research Libraries (ARL) that explores the issue of foreign acquisition and how it affects collection in international studies, area studies, collection development, and practices of international research libraries.*

53. *Collection Development in a Digital Environment,* edited by Sul H. Lee (Vol. 28, No. 1, 1999). *Explores ethical and technological dilemmas of collection development and gives several suggestions on how a library can successfully deal with these challenges and provide patrons with the information they need.*

54. *Collection Management: Preparing Today's Bibliographers for Tomorrow's Libraries,* edited by Karen Rupp-Serrano, MLS, MPA (Vol. 28, No. 2, 1999). *For both beginners and professional,* Collection Development *addresses your vexing questions that librarians continually face to assist you in creating a cost-effective and resourceful library.*

55. *The Age Demographics of Academic Librarians: A Profession Apart,* edited by Stanley J. Wilder (Vol. 28, No. 3, 1999). *The average age of librarians has been increasing dramatically since 1990. This unique book will provide insights on how this demographic issue can impact a library and what can be done to make the effects positive.*

56. *Collection Development in the Electronic Environment: Shifting Priorities,* edited by Sul H. Lee (Vol. 28, No. 4, 1999). *Through case studies and firsthand experiences, this volume discusses meeting the needs of scholars at universities, budgeting issues, user education, staffing in the electronic age, collaborating libraries and resources, and how vendors meet the needs of different customers.*

57. *Library Training for Staff and Customers,* edited by Sara Ramser Beck, MLS, MBA (Vol. 29, No. 1, 1999). *This comprehensive book is designed to assist library professionals involved in presenting or planning training for library staff members and customers. You will explore ideas for effective general reference training, training on automated systems, training in specialized subjects such as African American history and biography, and training for areas such as patents and trademarks, and business subjects.* Library Training for Staff and Customers *answers numerous training questions and is an excellent guide for planning staff development.*

58. *Integration in the Library Organization,* edited by Christine E. Thompson, PhD (Vol. 29, No. 2, 1999). *Provides librarians with the necessary tools to help libraries balance and integrate public and technical services and to improve the capability of libraries to offer patrons quality services and large amounts of information.*

59. *Management for Research Libraries Cooperation,* edited by Sul H. Lee (Vol. 29, No. 3/4, 2000). *Delivers sound advice, models, and strategies for increasing sharing between institutions to maximize the amount of printed and electronic research material you can make available in your library while keeping costs under control.*

60. *Academic Research on the Internet: Options for Scholars & Libraries,* edited by Helen Laurence, MLS, EdD, and William Miller, PhD, MLS (Vol. 30, No. 1/2/3/4, 2000) *"Emphasizes quality over quantity. . . . Presents the reader with the best research-oriented Web sites in the field. A state-of-the-art review of academic use of the Internet as well as a guide to the best Internet sites and services. . . . A useful addition for any academic library." (David A. Tyckoson, MLS, Head of Reference, California State University, Fresno)*

61. *Research Collections and Digital Information,* edited by Sul H. Lee (Vol. 31, No. 2, 2000). *Offers new strategies for collecting, organizing, and accessing library materials in the digital age.*

62. *Off-Campus Library Services,* edited by Ann Marie Casey (Vol. 31, No. 3/4, 2001 and Vol. 32, No. 1/2, 2001). *This informative volume examines various aspects of off-campus, or distance learning. It explores training issues for library staff, Web site development, changing roles for librarians, the uses of conferencing software, library support for Web-based courses, library agreements and how to successfully negotiate them, and much more!*

63. *Leadership in the Library and Information Science Professions: Theory and Practice,* edited by Mark D. Winston, MLS, PhD (Vol. 32, No. 3/4, 2001). *Offers fresh ideas for developing and using leadership skills, including recruiting potential leaders, staff training and development, issues of gender and ethnic diversity, and budget strategies for success.*

64. *Diversity Now: People, Collections, and Services in Academic Libraries,* edited by Teresa Y. Neely, PhD, and Kuang-Hwei (Janet) Lee-Smeltzer, MS, MSLIS (Vol. 33, No. 1/2/3/4, 2001). *Examines multicultural trends in academic libraries' staff and users, types of collections, and services offered.*

65. *Libraries and Electronic Resources: New Partnerships, New Practices, New Perspectives,* edited by Pamela L. Higgins (Vol. 35, No. 1/2, 2001). *An essential guide to the Internet's impact on electronic resources management–past, present, and future.*

66. *Impact of Digital Technology on Library Collections and Resource Sharing,* edited by Sul H. Lee (Vol. 35, No. 3, 2001). *Shows how digital resources have changed the traditional academic library.*

67. *Evaluating the Twenty-First Century Library: The Association of Research Libraries New Measures Initiative, 1997-2001,* edited by Donald L. DeWitt, PhD (Vol. 35, No. 4, 2001). *This collection of articles (thirteen of which previously appeared in ARL's bimonthly newsletter/report on research issues and actions) examines the Association of Research Libraries' "new measures" initiative.*

68. *Information Literacy Programs: Successes and Challenges,* edited by Patricia Durisin, MLIS (Vol. 36, No. 1/2, 2002). *Examines Web-based collaboration, teamwork with academic and administrative colleagues, evidence-based librarianship, and active learning strategies in library instruction programs.*

69. *Electronic Resources and Collection Development,* edited by Sul H. Lee (Vol. 36, No. 3, 2002). *Shows how electronic resources have impacted traditional collection development policies and practices.*

70. *Distance Learning Library Services: The Tenth Off-Campus Library Services Conference,* edited by Patrick B. Mahoney (Vol. 37, No. 1/2/3/4, 2002). *Explores the pitfalls of providing information services to distance students and suggests ways to avoid them.*

71. *The Strategic Stewardship of Cultural Resources: To Preserve and Protect,* edited by Andrea T. Merrill, BA (Vol. 38, No. 1/2/3/4, 2003). *Leading library, museum, and archival professionals share their expertise on a wide variety of preservation and security issues.*

72. *The Twenty-First Century Art Librarian,* edited by Terrie L. Wilson, MLS (Vol. 39, No. 1, 2003). *"A must-read addition to every art, architecture, museum, and visual resources library bookshelf." (Betty Jo Irvine, PhD, Fine Arts Librarian, Indiana University)*

73. *Digital Images and Art Libraries in the Twenty-First Century,* edited by Susan Wyngaard, MLS (Vol. 39, No. 2/3, 2003). *Provides an in-depth look at the technology that art librarians must understand in order to work effectively in today's digital environment.*

74. *Improved Access to Information: Portals, Content Selection, and Digital Information,* edited by Sul H. Lee (Vol. 39, No. 4, 2003). *Examines how improved electronic resources can allow libraries to provide an increasing amount of digital information to an ever-expanding patron base.*

75. *The Changing Landscape for Electronic Resources: Content, Access, Delivery, and Legal Issues,* edited by Yem S. Fong, MLS, and Suzanne M. Ward, MA (Vol. 40, No. 1/2, 2004). *Focuses on various aspects of electronic resources for libraries, including statewide resource-sharing initiatives, licensing issues, open source software, standards, and scholarly publishing.*

Print vs. Digital:
The Future of Coexistence

Sul H. Lee
Editor

Print vs. Digital: The Future of Coexistence has been co-published simultaneously as *Journal of Library Administration*, Volume 46, Number 2 2007.

Routledge
Taylor & Francis Group
NEW YORK AND LONDON

First Published by

The Haworth Information Press®, 10 Alice Street, Binghamton, NY 13904-1580 USA

Transferred to Digital Printing 2009 by Routledge
711 Third Avenue, New York, NY 10017
2 Park Square, Milton Park, Abingdon, Oxon, OX14 4RN

Print vs. Digital: The Future of Coexistence has been co-published simultaneously as *Journal of Library Administration®*, Volume 46, Number 2 2007.

Routledge is an imprint of the Taylor & Francis Group, an informa business

First issued in paperback 2016

The development, preparation, and publication of this work has been undertaken with great care. However, the publisher, employees, editors, and agents of The Haworth Press and all imprints of The Haworth Press, Inc., including The Haworth Medical Press® and Pharmaceutical Products Press®, are not responsible for any errors contained herein or for consequences that may ensue from use of materials or information contained in this work. With regard to case studies, identities and circumstances of individuals discussed herein have been changed to protect confidentiality. Any resemblance to actual persons, living or dead, is entirely coincidental.

The Haworth Press is committed to the dissemination of ideas and information according to the highest standards of intellectual freedom and the free exchange of ideas. Statements made and opinions expressed in this publication do not necessarily reflect the views of the Publisher, Directors, management, or staff of The Haworth Press, Inc., or an endorsement by them.

Cover design by Jennifer M. Gaska.

Library of Congress Cataloging-in-Publication Data

Print vs. digital : the future of coexistence / Sul H. Lee, editor.
     p. cm.
     "Co-published simultaneously as Journal of library administration, volume 46, number 2."
     Includes bibliographical references and index.

     1. Academic libraries–Collection development. 2. Research libraries–Collection development. 3. Libraries–Special collections–Electronic information resources. 4. Scholarly publishing. 5. Electronic journals. 6. Libraries and students. 7. Libraries and scholars. 8. Libraries and the Internet. 9. Communication in learning and scholarship. I. Lee, Sul H. II. Journal of library administration. III. Title: Print versus digital.
Z675.U5P865 2007
  025.2'1877–dc22

                                               2006029990

Publisher's Note
The publisher has gone to great lengths to ensure the quality of this reprint but points out that some imperfections in the original may be apparent.

ISBN13: 978-0-7890-3575-2 (hbk)
ISBN13: 978-1-138-99528-4 (pbk)

This section provides you with a list of major indexing & abstracting services and other tools for bibliographic access. That is to say, each service began covering this periodical during the year noted in the right column. Most Websites which are listed below have indicated that they will either post, disseminate, compile, archive, cite or alert their own Website users with research-based content from this work. (This list is as current as the copyright date of this publication.)

Abstracting, Website/Indexing Coverage . . . . Year When Coverage Began

- *(IBR) International Bibliography of Book Reviews on the Humanities and Social Sciences (Thomson) <http://www.saur.de>* 2006
- *(IBZ) International Bibliography of Periodical Literature on the Humanities and Social Sciences (Thomson) <http://www.saur.de>* 1995
- **Academic Search Premier (EBSCO)** *<http://search.ebscohost.com>* 2006
- **Business ASAP (Thomson Gale)** 1994
- **Business ASAP- International (Thomson Gale)** 1984
- **Business Source Complete (EBSCO)** *<http://search.ebscohost.com>* 2006
- **Business Source Premier (EBSCO)** *<http://search.ebscohost.com>* 2006
- **General BusinessFile ASAP (Thomson Gale)** 1993
- **General BusinessFile ASAP- International (Thomson Gale)** 1984
- **General Reference Center GOLD (Thomson Gale)** 1984
- **General Reference Center INTERNATIONAL (Thomson Gale)** 1984
- **InfoTrac Custom (Thomson Gale)** 1996
- **InfoTrac OneFile (Thomson Gale)** 1984
- **INSPEC (The Institution of Engineering and Technology)** *<http://www.iee.org.uk/publish/>* 1986
- **LISA: Library and Information Science Abstracts (ProQuest CSA)** *<http://www.csa.com/factsheets/list-set-c.php>* 1989
- **MasterFILE Premier (EBSCO)** *<http://search.ebscohost.com>* 1993
- **Professional Development Collection (Thomson Gale)** 2006
- *Academic Search Alumni Edition (EBSCO) <http://search.ebscohost.com>* 2007

(continued)

(continued)

(continued)

Bibliographic Access

- *Magazines for Libraries (Katz)*

- *MediaFinder <http://www.mediafinder.com/>*

- *Ulrich's Periodicals Directory: The Global Source for Periodicals Information Since 1932 <http://www.bowkerlink.com>*

Special Bibliographic Notes related to special journal issues (separates) and indexing/abstracting:

- indexing/abstracting services in this list will also cover material in any "separate" that is co-published simultaneously with Haworth's special thematic journal issue or DocuSerial. Indexing/abstracting usually covers material at the article/chapter level.
- monographic co-editions are intended for either non-subscribers or libraries which intend to purchase a second copy for their circulating collections.
- monographic co-editions are reported to all jobbers/wholesalers/approval plans. The source journal is listed as the "series" to assist the prevention of duplicate purchasing in the same manner utilized for books-in-series.
- to facilitate user/access services all indexing/abstracting services are encouraged to utilize the co-indexing entry note indicated at the bottom of the first page of each article/chapter/contribution.
- this is intended to assist a library user of any reference tool (whether print, electronic, online, or CD-ROM) to locate the monographic version if the library has purchased this version but not a subscription to the source journal.
- individual articles/chapters in any Haworth publication are also available through the Haworth Document Delivery Service (HDDS).

As part of
Haworth's
continuing
commitment
to better serve
our library
patrons,
we are
proud to
be working
with the
following
electronic
services:

AGGREGATOR SERVICES

EBSCOhost

Ingenta

J-Gate

Minerva

OCLC FirstSearch   FirstSearch

Oxmill

SwetsWise

LINK RESOLVER SERVICES

1Cate (Openly Informatics)

ChemPort
(American Chemical Society)

CrossRef

Gold Rush (Coalliance)

LinkOut (PubMed)

LINKplus (Atypon)

LinkSolver (Ovid)

LinkSource with A-to-Z (EBSCO)

Resource Linker (Ulrich)

SerialsSolutions (ProQuest)

SFX (Ex Libris)

Sirsi Resolver (SirsiDynix)

Tour (TDnet)

Vlink (Extensity, formerly Geac)

WebBridge (Innovative Interfaces)

Print vs. Digital: The Future of Coexistence

CONTENTS

ABOUT THE EDITOR

Sul H. Lee is Peggy V. Helmerich Chair and professor of Library and Information Studies at the University of Oklahoma and dean of University of Oklahoma Libraries. Professor Lee has taught in the School of Library and Information Sciences and directs a major university research library with a collection exceeding 4.5 million volumes. He has served as professor and dean at the University of Oklahoma since 1978 and is the senior dean on the University of Oklahoma campus in Norman, Oklahoma.

Professor Lee's academic background is in political science, international relations, and library and information science and he holds graduate degrees in these disciplines. He is author of more than two dozen books in the field of librarianship, along with numerous articles and professional presentations. In addition to his current positions at the University of Oklahoma, Professor Lee has taught at Oxford University in Oxford, England and the University of Michigan. He is internationally recognized as a consultant on libraries and has served on important national and regional professional organizations and consortiums such as the Association of Research Libraries board of directors; the board of governors for the Research Libraries Group (RLG); the Council of the American Library Association; and as chair of the Greater Midwest Research Library Consortium.

He is also editor-in-chief for The Haworth Press's academic journal division and editor of Haworth's *Journal of Library Administration*. He serves regularly as consultant to library service providers, academic book vendors, publishers, and advises state and local governments on library affairs. His outstanding career spans more than 40 years in academic libraries and he has witnessed the transition of libraries from the era of card catalogs to the proliferation and general acceptance of digital information.

For Melissa

Introduction

As I consider the title of this collection of papers, *Print vs. Digital: The Future of Coexistence*, I am reminded of a statement made more than 20 years ago by Vartan Gregorian, the well-known professor of history, university president, and president of the New York Public Library. When asked about libraries and digital technology Dr. Gregorian, who had just overseen the conversion of New York Public's card catalog to an online version, replied, "The book is here to stay. What we're doing is symbolic of the peaceful coexistence of the book and the computer."[1] What I believe Gregorian meant was that the traditional book and digital information are permanent fixtures of the contemporary research library, and that librarians value both and want, above all, to acquire, preserve, and offer both print and electronic resources to those who use libraries.

That is an admirable goal and one that most 21st century librarians accept as a matter of course. I have learned, however, that it is very necessary for academic library administrators to build a sound working relationship between those who oversee traditional print resources and digital information within their libraries. Building such a relationship, or how academic libraries can reach a comfortable coexistence between traditional print and digital resources, is the theme of the articles that follow.

As most of us already know, balancing print and digital resources in academic libraries is not an easy task, neither is it always a comfortable one. While I think we all will admit that change in our profession brought on by the availability of electronic resources is well underway, we do not always agree about the pace that this change should take. We

[Haworth co-indexing entry note]: "Introduction." Lee, Sul H. Co-published simultaneously in *Journal of Library Administration* (The Haworth Information Press, an imprint of The Haworth Press, Inc.) Vol. 46, No. 2, 2007, pp. 1-2; and: *Print vs. Digital: The Future of Coexistence* (ed: Sul H. Lee) The Haworth Information Press, an imprint of The Haworth Press, Inc., 2007, pp. 1-2. Single or multiple copies of this article are available for a fee from The Haworth Document Delivery Service [1-800-HAWORTH, 9:00 a.m. - 5:00 p.m. (EST). E-mail address: docdelivery@haworthpress.com].

Available online at http://jla.haworthpress.com
doi:10.1300/J111v46n02_01

are fortunate, though, to have eight nationally recognized experts in contemporary librarianship offer their views on the possibilities for co-existence between traditional and electronic resources. I am confident that we may find grounds for a peaceful coexistence between digital and print information in the following articles. The discussions range from observations about the changing behavior of the 21st century consumer of information resources to a bold announcement that the end of print journals is upon us. I greatly appreciate the opportunity to present these papers in both journal and monograph formats and hope that readers may find the different perspectives new and enlightening.

Sul H. Lee
Editor

NOTE

1. *Time*, February 25, 1985, p. 94.

The Impact of Evolving Information-Seeking Behaviors Upon Research Libraries: A Case Study

Fred Heath

SUMMARY. Rapid developments in information technologies have impacted scholarly communication, teaching, and learning in fundamental ways. The time-honored practice of a community of scholars gathering on a single campus to pursue a common research interest is being challenged as the symbol of university research. In its stead there has emerged world-wide discipline-centered scholarship where collaboration and synergy are dependent upon the Internet and the World Wide Web. New research methods mine universes of data vastly deeper and richer than the print world enabled, extend inquiry into data structures more complex than the book and the journal, and give rise to new meanings of the notion of "original sources." Student learning and student behaviors are also evolving. The evident GenX penchants–for multi-tasking and group collaboration, for electronic information and self-sufficiency–also bring new challenges to all of those on campus who share

Fred Heath is Vice Provost and Director, University of Texas Libraries, University of Texas at Austin, P.O. Box P–21st and Speedway, Austin, TX 78713-8916 (E-mail: fheath@austin.utexas.edu).

[Haworth co-indexing entry note]: "The Impact of Evolving Information-Seeking Behaviors Upon Research Libraries: A Case Study." Heath, Fred. Co-published simultaneously in *Journal of Library Administration* (The Haworth Information Press, an imprint of The Haworth Press, Inc.) Vol. 46, No. 2, 2007, pp. 3-16; and: *Print vs. Digital: The Future of Coexistence* (ed: Sul H. Lee) The Haworth Information Press, an imprint of The Haworth Press, Inc., 2007, pp. 3-16. Single or multiple copies of this article are available for a fee from The Haworth Document Delivery Service [1-800-HAWORTH, 9:00 a.m. - 5:00 p.m. (EST). E-mail address: docdelivery@haworthpress.com].

Available online at http://jla.haworthpress.com

doi:10.1300/J111v46n02_02

responsibilities in the increasingly complex learning space that the university itself has become. This paper reflects on some of the efforts of one research library to respond to the pressures of the digital age while sustaining its efforts to build enduring repositories of the human record. doi:10.1300/J111v46n02_02 *[Article copies available for a fee from The Haworth Document Delivery Service: 1-800-HAWORTH. E-mail address: <docdelivery@haworthpress.com> Website: <http://www.HaworthPress. com> © 2007 by The Haworth Press, Inc. All rights reserved.]*

KEYWORDS. Research behaviors, research and World Wide Web, university students and library usage, search terminology, search techniques, University of Texas, undergraduate library, closure of research libraries

PURPOSE

Good afternoon. I am pleased to be here with you today to discuss the complex issue of evolving information-seeking behaviors in the digital age. The issue has many different facets, and I hope that I will be able to touch on a number of them today. My perspective will be that of a director of a large research library, and my methodology will be that of the case study. The perspective should be self-evident. All of you know the University of Texas as a large research university–until January 4 of this year, one better known for its academics than its athletic programs. The methodology may merit explanation. I suspect the proximate reason that I am here today has something to do with the notoriety that I and the University of Texas have achieved in blog space as a result of the decision to close our Undergraduate Library. In case you are new to the library world, or are otherwise massively disinterested in the topic, I should tell you that we opened the fall semester at the University of Texas without the Undergraduate Library that had served us well for forty years. For the most part, the established press took a balanced view of the situation and exhibited a rather nuanced understanding of the factors that played into our decision–as did our university community generally. But the blogs and the e-press often reacted more viscerally.

- "Last Books Evicted from UT Undergrad Library" wrote one from his e-forum.

- "Say bye-bye to the books, kids" wrote another to a readership of unknown size.
- Though my favorite was "We Don't Need no Stinkin' Books."

And so, this venue affords me a welcome forum to address *learning behaviors* and *library as place* from the perspective of one research university addressing teaching and learning effectiveness in an evolving and increasingly complex landscape. The case study I will share with you today, is, if you will, an opportunity to set the record straight as to how that decision process unfolded.

However, this occasion means much more to me than that. At the University of Texas, I have the opportunity to work with an outstanding cadre of technology and library leaders. The people with whom I work: Tom Staley and Betty Sue Flowers, Don Carlton and Roy Mersky, Dan Updegrove and Andrew Dillon are well known for their leadership in our overlapping areas of the broader information profession. And over my shoulder loom the legacies of Nettie Lee Benson, Harry Ransom, Brooke Sheldon, Harold Billings, and many others. Together, legions of dedicated people have built one of the great research libraries in the world. And today, the current leadership is engaged in a Presidential initiative to host an invited symposium in the Fall on just what it means to be, and what it will require to remain, a great research library in the unfolding of the twenty-first century. It is a library director's dream to have such an initiative conceived and funded at the presidential level. My colleagues and I are grateful for the opportunity it represents. Currently, we are shaping the agenda for that symposium, and this forum offers the opportunity for me to put my thoughts to paper, and to listen to my esteemed colleagues, to gain important information that will assist us in that effort.

My research focus, as a librarian, is based upon the LibQUAL+™ protocol. We have spent quite a few years developing that tool, and are gratified to witness its growing acceptance across the world. In our work, we measure and assess how library service quality is defined in the research university environment–and increasingly in other libraries–not only in North America, but globally. To date, over 700 libraries have participated in the LibQUAL+ assessment at least once, here and in Europe. There is growing interest in the protocol in Asia, in Africa, and in South America. In that context, it is my practice to address trends, to look at the issues relating to shifting information-seeking behaviors *in the aggregate*. Today, the case study approach will ground my observations in *the particular*, but I hope you will find them useful to you as you consider some of these same issues from your local perspective. The aggregate is, after all, nothing but the sum of our local experiences.

And finally, I want to thank Karen Hunter, who joins us here this week, for inviting me to present at the Elsevier program last month in San Antonio during the American Library Association Mid-Winter meeting. Preparation for that program was another opportunity for me to shape the ideas I will share with you today.

I will talk a bit about the process involved in the decision by the University of Texas Libraries to close its Undergraduate Library and to repurpose that facility, in collaboration with other stakeholders, into what we hope will evolve into a digital learning commons. To our mind, the digital commons, when realized, will enable students and faculty to work with librarians, technology experts, teaching experts with skills in electronic learning, and others to harness the promises of the rapid advances in the digital arena to enable more effective teaching and learning.

With an eye on the clock, I am going to take you on a tour of four different aspects of the decision process:

- *Realities.* First of all, the differences between some perceptions of what has occurred and the directions the University of Texas may be perceived to be heading will be contrasted with the actual state of affairs. Behind some of the more virulent headlines and some of the more heated blog rants is a story that is at once more complex and probably less interesting than might appear at first encounter.
- *Economic Factors.* Secondly, I'll address some of the underlying factors that contributed to the decision to close the Undergraduate Library. Both historical factors and current realities contributed to the decision we made, as I hope you will be able to see.
- *Sustainability.* Additionally, I want to make it clear that issues central to the role of the research library in the core teaching and learning missions were at work. We want to make certain that other campus agencies with student learning and teaching effectiveness missions see the University of Texas Libraries as key collaborators whose skill sets could complement and extend their own.
- *Behavioral Shifts.* And finally, we were also motivated to engineer effective responses to what we perceive as significant behavioral shifts in information seeking. The way students pursue the acquisition of information is undergoing fundamental transformation, as is the way faculty teach, and the way all of higher education communicates.

REALITIES

The Flawn Academic Center, or FAC, is a five floor building of some 130,000 square feet, constructed in the 1960s. Well before the beginning of the past academic year, Information Technology Services (ITS) had displaced the University of Texas Libraries as the dominant tenant of the FAC. The Vice President for ITS maintains his operational office in FAC. Another major operational unit, the Division of Instructional Innovation and Assessment (DIIA) also maintains its primary offices there, as do the directors of the Accessibility Institute and the Undergraduate Writing Center.

Over a period of several decades, the library footprint in the building had shrunk. The library surrendered square footage to space starved units from other parts of campus. Over time, the library collections initially designed to serve the undergraduate population shriveled from some 200,000 volumes on two floors, to perhaps ninety thousand volumes that occupied about 6,000 square feet of the third level. As a consequence of the relentless pressures for space on a burgeoning university campus, the Flawn Academic Center slowly lost its programmatic integrity.

Over the last quarter of the twentieth century, as programmatic focus blurred, FAC became an academic hostel, serving as the domicile of opportunity for a host of campus functions. As it lost coherence and the advocacy that a primary occupant provides, the building began showing its age, with a weary infrastructure and frayed furnishings. Electrical supply failed to keep pace with the demands of the technological advances of the late decades of the twentieth century. There were, for example, few opportunities for students to power up their many electronic tools: laptops, cell phones, PDAs, iPods, and the like. It was anything but a Net Generation-friendly place. The Flawn Academic Center was a tired facility with an uncertain purpose, a situation that did little to honor the name of the distinguished living former President whose name it bore.

Yet, the building occupied a prime real estate footprint on campus, bounded on one side by the historic University Tower (the signature building of the University of Texas), and on the other by the Texas Union. FAC opens onto a vibrant student mall, shaded by regal live oaks and the site of most outdoor student free speech and organizational activities. It was also the open volume preferred by vast numbers of students on a daily basis. Open on almost a "seven by twenty-four" basis, it was frequented by more than 150,000 students a month, a use exceeded only by Perry Castañeda Library, whose entry gates recorded some 200,000 monthly visits.

The erosion of that fine building gave pause to all administrators who shared teaching and learning missions in its space. Among us, the feeling emerged that should the building have a single programmatic purpose in service to student learning, should we recapture the student-centeredness that once defined the structure, we would have the opportunity to encourage interested donors to restore the building, endow the program, and associate his or her name with the iconic Peter Flawn. The future we believed was in collaborative effort.

ECONOMIC FACTORS

Additional economic factors were in play that raised questions about the desirability of the University of Texas Libraries maintaining an operation that was no longer as central to the educational mission as it was at the time of its creation.

One example may serve to illustrate the issue. There are fixed costs to maintaining a full-fledged circulating collection in a library that scales to 200,000 volumes. Even at 90,000 volumes, the holdings of the UGL exceeded the median number of titles in North America's 3,500 colleges and universities. I understand better the reaction in the library blogs, now that I know that half of institutions of higher education in the United States hold 70,000 volumes or fewer. To sustain the selection of these titles, to circulate the volumes, to re-shelve them and maintain the stacks, the University of Texas Libraries deployed a workforce of some 14 benefit-eligible employees and a considerable additional FTE in student workers. The payroll dedicated to this function amounted to some $500,000 annually. As our cost studies showed, the return on investment for this effort was inefficient. Were the University of Texas Libraries to maintain similar collection maintenance/staffing ratios across all of its collections and libraries, circulation and stack maintenance functions alone would amount to considerably more than the personnel costs of all library operations at the present time.

Now, libraries are conservative organizations, notoriously slow to change. Had there not been external impetus, the cost factors may not have been addressed so abruptly, and the service to students could have continued unchanged and unaddressed into some distant time. But there was an external impetus. In 2003, the state of Texas elected a new governor who rode the rhetoric of fiscal responsibility to a solid victory.

Upon taking up residency in the Governor's mansion, he issued an Executive Order that rolled back the approved state budget for FY 2004 by 5% for every state agency and institution. In an understandable and courageous decision, the University of Texas library administration in place at the time elected to sustain the library collections budget by absorbing the five percent rollback on the personnel side. As I came into the library in August 2003, shortly before the new budget year was to begin, retirements, incentives for earlier retirement, and lost vacant positions largely covered the $1,000,000 impact that the Governor's mandate represented for the personnel budget of the University of Texas Libraries.

The effects of an exigency-driven personnel reduction on our libraries were, of course, random and, in some cases, devastating. The impact was especially harsh, as it was executed under a tight deadline. There was little opportunity to manage the personnel re-structuring centrally. Vacated positions fell randomly. Some units were forced to limp along in severely understaffed situations, while we scrambled to redistribute our talent. During the course of fiscal years 2004 and 2005 we were able to realize some economies, re-engineer some programs, and to partially repair some of the deficits. But problems remained.

The decision to close the UGL helped to ameliorate that impact. Elimination of collection management functions in the Undergraduate Library allowed us over the course of the Summer 2005 to reassign the staff involved in that function (along with the student wages) and to further redress service issues created by the rescission. Through this move, we were able to take many of our other units back to their 2003 staffing levels. Most of the volumes in the Undergraduate Library were reassigned to the main library. There, the impact upon circulation and stack management functions was minimal and the functions were absorbed with little personnel augmentation. The electronic reserves and modest print reserve function of UGL was merged with PCL; its staffing component accompanied the transfer.

SUSTAINABILITY

So, thus far you have learned that the act was less sensational than presaged by some of the more reckless headlines. No books were pulped, discarded, or otherwise abused. The number of libraries was simply reduced by one, and the relatively small collection of books in that facility made their way to the stacks of other libraries where they nestled up alongside eight million of their companions–by some counts the sixth largest library collection in North America. No staff were released. Instead, relocated employees were enthusiastically welcomed into their new places of employment. In some cases they brought needed new skills; in other cases they were able to shore up staffing deficits visited upon us by the Governor's rescission.

But the part of the story that is perhaps controversial is a feeling on my part, shared by the management team, that the Undergraduate Library as it was configured at the University of Texas had become an anachronism, and was no longer serving its earlier vital role in undergraduate student learning. This is a contentious statement, and unless I am careful in my explication, I risk offending the very talented staff who worked in the Undergraduate Library, and perhaps some of my colleagues in ARL who have elected to continue to support–for very valid reasons–similar resources on their own campus. I will attempt to explain our perspective.

I think most of us here today would agree that the notion of Undergraduate Libraries evolved in the pre-computerized era of the 1950s and 1960s, when American research universities rode the floodtide of postwar economic prosperity, record student enrollments, and soaring public confidence to new heights. Research libraries grew rapidly; and public university libraries grew at an unprecedented pace. By the 1960s, the University of Texas Main Library, in the University Tower, had extended the shelving capacity of that edifice to some two million volumes. And the riches continued to pour into the University of Texas, eventually reaching today's count in excess of eight million volumes.

But those volumes were not equally accessible to all at the University of Texas. For, as was the case with most libraries of the time, the intellectual storehouse represented by those books was cordoned off behind closed stacks. The closed stacks collections were accessible only to faculty and graduate students.

The burgeoning undergraduate population met their class and research assignments by queuing up at the service desk, waiting until their number was called, turning in their call slips, and waiting again for the seemingly interminable process of paging to run its course. And what informed search strategy did an undergraduate manage to construct on those call slips?

From my early days as an undergraduate at Tulane University I recall that my call slips were in the large part amateurish and uninformed. Invariably, large numbers of the volumes I paged were unceremoniously dumped into the return slot within moments of their eventual delivery to me from the stacks.

Undergraduate libraries, such as ours at the University of Texas, emerged during the 1960s to remedy just such problems. The undergraduate library was to be "a building of their own," where clueless, swarming undergraduates such as myself were removed from the midst of "scholars." The undergraduate library lightened the load on main library paging staff, and contributed to the restoration of the "right" decorum in that province of the faculty. For the undergraduates, there was crafted a small, carefully selected collection, modeled, often as not, on the notion of the "western canon," exposing undergraduates everywhere to the "right" ideas.

The undergraduate library, its collection a handpicked subset of the information universe, may have helped overcome the state of information illiteracy in the student body. Where undergraduate libraries existed, students of my era achieved a rudimentary level of success by browsing the carefully chosen open collections and networking out from the bibliographies of those texts to other sources. We slowly honed our bibliographic skills as we pursued our assignments. And thus there was a brief "season in the sun" for the undergraduate library as it performed several important social and intellectual roles on the campuses of America's research universities.

But, in my estimation, the season of the undergraduate library was a short one. It is interesting in retrospect how relentless social change, including the student revolution of the Vietnam and civil rights era scraped away the concept of a "canon" to which "right" thought must conform. The notion of "right thinking" had little relevance to students who crowded America's campuses to avoid supporting with their lives a notoriously unpopular war and who lent their voices in protest to social injustice at home.

But in my judgment, it was not the Vietnam War, or social change, that eroded the relevance of the undergraduate library. It was the progress we were making in librarianship itself. In the 1970s, for philosophical and economic reasons, large research universities began to adopt the architectural concept of large, open-stack, main libraries. At the University of Texas, the massive Perry-Castañeda Library (PCL as we call it) was opened during that time. A formidable structure, it was, and is, an exhilarating mixture of open stack repositories of the human record, and nooks and crannies where the researcher can pursue his or her intellectual quests in concentrated quiet. With the opening of the Perry Castañeda Library in 1977, the undergraduate was no longer obliged to construct a world view based only on a small sliver of the university's vast riches. Rather, as curious as he or she was uninformed, the undergraduate student was free to browse and otherwise access a vastly expanded universe.

With the opening of PCL, I would suggest, the Undergraduate Library at the University of Texas lost one of its most important reasons for being. Students no longer needed the small browsing collection. The position of the academic library was further eroded in the 1980s when the bibliographic hurdles confronting the undergraduate began to be cut away with advancement in information technologies. By the mid-1980s we had useful, almost intuitive, on-line public catalogs, which facilitated intellectual access to the increasingly complex labyrinth of printed books.

And as the undergraduate library's reason for being evanesced, the collections in the undergraduate library began to lose their focus. The idea of a "canon" lost credence, and faded away. Undergraduate library budgets were reduced and reallocated to more pressing research needs. Undergraduate library collection sizes were reduced to find room for other programs.

By the mid-1990s, with the advent of the World Wide Web and the resultant broad access to electronic databases, reference tools, and electronic journals, the undergraduate library sometimes became simply another undifferentiated public space, maintained in its existing configuration by the forces of inertia and custom. But, certainly, at the University of Texas, the FAC/UGL remained a popular gathering space, meeting place, and "getaway" for personal study.

THE DECISION MATRIX

And so, in the confluence of all of these factors, it became apparent that the University of Texas Libraries could, and should, re-direct its considerable investment in the undergraduate library. But we could only do that if we could resolve one very perplexing issue: how could we divest ourselves of that investment, and still maintain a "7 by 24" community gathering space that the UGL had become? That our students had come to expect?

How could we do that? It was piercingly clear to the library management team that we could only achieve that outcome by partnering with others whose missions overlapped with our own in the student learning environment, and only if we could craft a mission that enabled us to capture the synergies among those overlapping responsibilities and allowed each of us to leverage the opportunity that collaboration represented.

Had we the time today, we could talk about the unique aspects each collaborator brought to the undertaking, and the benefits each would derive. For our purposes here, we will talk only about the benefits the libraries derived.

One important role played by the Undergraduate Library was as home to our library instruction program. Not surprisingly, our instruction librarians at the University of Texas are very good. And their role is appreciated by the faculty they serve and the students they reach. But, sadly, on our campus of 50,000 students, the library instruction mission as conceived and executed could not be scaled. With a small core staff of professionals and generous participation by librarians in the reference and bibliographer ranks, we have been able to achieve about 1,000 classroom instruction sessions annually. Unfortunately, on an annual basis, the University of Texas offers more than 23,000 course sections each year. The model of one librarian in one classroom for each course section once a semester was far beyond our reach.

And so we began to ask ourselves. How could we achieve scale through synergy?

- Could we perhaps partner in the digital environment with DIIA, ITS, the Writing Center, the Accessibility Institute and professors and students in the School of Information and thus extend our reach?
- Could Blackboard and Sakai, our course management alternatives, offer digital options, such as subject modules developed by librarians and selectively applied by faculty to their Blackboard spaces? And in this way could we further diffuse needed information literacy skills into the student body?

If we could achieve those outcomes, perhaps we could reach a greater number of students at their point of need. Certainly in all cases a digital module will not be an adequate substitute for librarian-as-teacher at the front of the classroom. But could we evolve other remedies as well? We have relocated our instructional librarians to the main library and have adjusted their numbers in an attempt to give them the bandwidth to explore these questions. And we asked:

- Could a Library IM presence on Blackboard, with a librarian available at the student's very moment of need, serve as an alternate teaching or access method?
- And could we entice the Information School to enter this learning with us, revamping its curriculum and placing its students in a new learning laboratory with us, DIIA, ITS, the Writing Center, and others?

We have only asked these question; we have not answered them. But we have eager new partners in a evolving laboratory space where we fully intend to work to advance information literacy, critical inquiry, and technological skill sets of our students. Already the other partners have contributed the resources to take up the staffing void we created by our departure. The FAC, freshened with new paint, new furnishings, and rehabilitated teaching spaces, remains the student extended-hour facility on mid-campus. We retain our media library presence in service to students and DIIA's teaching role, contribute hours to the main service island, and sustain one security shift. We are taking our first tentative steps toward the future.

BEHAVIORAL ISSUES

Let me turn finally to behavioral issues and discuss some of the other observations that led us to this initiative. We have employed two survey methods to learn more about our students' information-seeking behaviors and their building use habits.

- We employ the LibQUAL+™ protocol annually, and
- We conducted on-site surveys to learn just what students were doing specifically in the FAC and the Undergraduate Library.

From LibQUAL+ we learned that student prized the "Library as Place" resource that the FAC's extended-hour environment represented. And we learned that they placed less value on mediated services that the various providers made available there.

And from our site surveys, we learned that the students valued the FAC:

- More as a place to meet
- More as a place to study

- Less as a location for mediated or transactional services
- Less as a library frequented for its print collections

Armed with that information, and with suggestions as to how the building could be put to more effective programmatic use in the teaching and learning arena, the stakeholders and I visited with college Deans, and the Provost. I personally visited with and obtained the blessing of former President Peter Flawn. With those clearances, we turned to our own faculty and student advisory groups, and to the student elected leadership, and obtained their support for the transformation.

Not only was the student support unanimous, but they were active participants over the summer in the selection of the new furnishings for the public areas. We heeded their advice on the possible need of quiet spaces, and kept the adjacent Life Sciences library open later to answer that potential need. We opened a coffee shop.

To date, I can tell you that traffic in the FAC remains about the same as last year, with perhaps a slight increase in computer log-ins. And the year-to-date use of Perry Castañeda library has picked up a bit. Reference traffic at PCL however has increased almost 10 percent; and use of the IM site is picking up. Our coffee shop, Prufrock's, has opened to banner sales, and the library plaza has assumed a new vibrancy and life. I am happy to report that the library has received no complaints from undergraduates about the transformation of the FAC.

I can tell you that I have enjoyed broad support among my ARL director colleagues for efforts to explore the efficacy of these collaborative efforts in the learning spaces. And the support on campus has been very strong as well. And we enjoy total support among the student body. Students have repeatedly conveyed their approval of the breadth and quality of the types of spaces made available to them.

But let me conclude where I began. The pushback has been in our library world. In the blog space we heard disapproval of other librarians. Disapproval was strongest among librarians at the smaller colleges for whom 90,000 volumes exceeds, as I said, the median number of books in America's college and university libraries. Some have suggested that our efforts to explore collaborations in the learning space is a diminishment rather than an enhancement of the library's role. Some of our own librarians agreed with that assessment initially, and may still.

I am confident that we are not in uncharted territory. My colleagues and I have visited exemplary sites at the University of Georgia, Georgia Tech, Emory University, Stanford, Penn State University, and the University of Michigan that serve as aspirational models. I feel collaboration gives us our best chance at buttressing our role in the instructional space and gives us our best prospect of being perceived as vital partners in teaching and learning at the University of Texas. And in the bargain, it has strengthened our ability to support the research mission. We will soon add our nine millionth volume, and we continue to add some 160,000 volumes annually, 7th among North American research universities, even as we increase our investments in the digital resources an outstanding research university demands.

The question is, simply, how do we respond to the pressures upon us? I want to conclude my remarks by suggesting to you our perspective should be that of the of the fictional persona recently introduced to us by Bill Wulf, President of the National Academy of Engineering:

> *It's New Year's Day, 1895. My name is Hans. For seven genera-tions my family has made the finest buttons in the region, using the good local horn.*
>
> *Today I learned that the railroad is coming to our village. My friend Olaf says that cheap factory buttons will come on the trains, but they will never compete with my craftsmanship.*
>
> *I think he is right, and wrong. They will come, but they will com-pete with my buttons. I must make some choices. I can become a distributor for the new buttons, or I can invest in the machinery to make buttons and export them. Or, closest to my heart, I can refine my craft and sell exceptional buttons to the wealthy.*
>
> *My family's business is dead. I cannot stop the train; I must change.*[1]

NOTE

1. William A. Wulf. The Information Railroad is Coming. *Educause Review* January/February 2003. www.educause.edu/ir/library/pdf/erm0310.pdf.

doi:10.1300/J111v46n02_02

Beyond Coexistence:
Finding Synergies Between
Print Content and Digital Information

Joan K. Lippincott

SUMMARY. Print and digital resources can have creative and interesting relationships; they do not need to reside in separate worlds. Libraries can play a role in working with faculty and students in promoting use of print resources to create new digital products and can be partners in creating learning objects that incorporate primary source materials from the library. Librarians can use the digital environment to create exhibits, displays, and community activities that encourage the use of print materials from the library. These are some of the synergies that can be promoted through the combined use of print and digital resources. doi:10.1300/J111v46n02_03 *[Article copies available for a fee from The Haworth Document Delivery Service: 1-800-HAWORTH. E-mail address: <docdelivery@haworthpress.com> Website: <http://www.HaworthPress.com> © 2007 by The Haworth Press, Inc. All rights reserved.]*

KEYWORDS. Internet, digitization, digital environment, digital libraries, primary sources, promotion

Joan K. Lippincott is affiliated with the Coalition for Networked Information, 21 Dupont Circle, Suite 800, Washington, DC 20036 (E-mail: joan@cni.org).

[Haworth co-indexing entry note]: "Beyond Coexistence: Finding Synergies Between Print Content and Digital Information." Lippincott, Joan K. Co-published simultaneously in *Journal of Library Administration* (The Haworth Information Press, an imprint of The Haworth Press, Inc.) Vol. 46, No. 2, 2007, pp. 17-26; and: *Print vs. Digital: The Future of Coexistence* (ed: Sul H. Lee) The Haworth Information Press, an imprint of The Haworth Press, Inc., 2007, pp. 17-26. Single or multiple copies of this article are available for a fee from The Haworth Document Delivery Service [1-800-HAWORTH, 9:00 a.m. - 5:00 p.m. (EST). E-mail address: docdelivery@haworthpress.com].

Available online at http://jla.haworthpress.com
doi:10.1300/J111v46n02_03

INTRODUCTION

Print and digital resources can do much more than just coexist in libraries. There are many opportunities for libraries to develop creative linkages between traditional print resources and Internet resources and services, and each can leverage the exposure and use of the other. Typically, librarians think of print resources and Internet resources as two categories of information that either have totally separate identities and associated services or are related only when a digital resource has a direct Internet counterpart, as is the case with many journals. When librarians approach digitization projects, a major, and sometimes sole emphasis is on how to develop the most accurate digital representation of a print resource (such as a book, journal article, or manuscript) rather than envisioning, in addition, the broader opportunities of the digital environment. This paper explores the kinds of creative synergies between print resources and digital projects that are being developed or could be developed by librarians, faculty, students, and others.

One of the key purposes that libraries serve is to provide the resources, access, and environment for people to pursue their interests. In academe, this means that the library provides resources for faculty members' research and teaching and for students' learning related to coursework and to their general interests. How can libraries do a better job of encouraging members of their user community to take advantage of the rich resources, both in print and digital form, that the library offers as they pursue their academic work? Some of the answers lie in promoting the synergies between the print and digital realms. Exposing more users and potential users to the rich resources of the library, assisting users with creating new digital products based on print resources, and providing print resources that extend the learning experiences of online environments, are all strategies that promote the educational mission of universities.

SUPPORTING FACULTY RESEARCH AND CREATIVITY IN SCHOLARLY COMMUNICATION

Faculty are developing content-rich websites as extensions of their research products or as the primary product of research. These websites can bridge print or analog resources and digital resources. Humanities faculty, in particular, build web collections of resources that represent digitized items from Special Collections, including such materials as manuscripts and photos. One of the best-known examples is the Valley of the Shadows website <valley.vcdh.virginia.edu/> developed by historians at the University of Virginia. This project contains digitized resources from two towns, one Union, one Confederate, during the American Civil War. The materials include newspapers, diaries, letters, official records, and maps. The University of Virginia has developed an infrastructure to support faculty work in the digital environment, some of which is provided by the library and some by other campus units. This infrastructure supports scholarship through provision of the primary resources themselves as well as through the availability of hardware, software, digital storage space, and staff with expertise in digitization, standards, and preservation. Many historians at other academic institutions question how they could develop large-scale digital projects in their own areas of specialization. They believe that their own campuses lack a supporting infrastructure, including hardware and software support, the availability of collaborators to assist with technical issues such as standards and preservation, and an institutional commitment to provide stewardship for digital content and reward faculty for creation of digital products.

Librarians can't provide remedies to the entire spectrum of researchers' needs for support, but they can, at a minimum, examine whether providing support for faculty digital initiatives is the kind of work they should be engaging in today. If librarians are serious about their interest in working with faculty to help ensure that their digital projects adhere to standards and are housed in an infrastructure that will promote stewardship, e.g., an institutional repository, they need to have the resources to work with faculty, including dedicated staff time, expertise, digitizing equipment, and facilities in which to do collaborative work. Websites such as the Valley of the Shadow are rich resources for scholarship, teaching, and learning. They can create a desire in students to use primary resources in the study of history. Rather than diminishing interest in traditional resources, they can encourage their use. Librarians can leverage their Special Collections materials through partnerships with faculty and others to develop digitized collections that highlight local research interests and the instructional program of the university. The print collections and the digitized collections can be used to support and enhance each other.

While creation of websites is now commonplace, new forms of scholarship are emerging, blending text and digital information in new ways. *Vectors* is "a new international electronic journal that brings to-gether visionary scholars with cutting-edge designers and technologists to propose a thorough rethinking of the dynamic relationship of form to content in academic research, focusing on ways technology shapes, transforms and reconfigures social and cultural relations" <http://vectors. iml.annenberg.edu/>. In one article in the new journal, the author, a his-torian, created a visual composite of evidence, which she felt was the best way to represent the everyday lives of rural Tuscans in the fifteenth century. Included with the text are images that put together components of a number of paintings and other cultural artifacts to create a new im-age. For example, one image shows the way in which fields were culti-vated for various crops, the types of farm equipment used, and the costumes of peasants. Taking the images of physical artifacts and com-bining them in new ways using digital technologies provides enhance-ments to scholarship. The analog resources are used as the basis for new, digital products of scholarship; they are re-mixed to highlight con-cepts or develop a theme. This kind of re-mixing is a hallmark of a style of creativity on the web, characterized as the "remix culture."[1] Librari-ans and other information professionals can be important collaborators in such projects, assisting researchers in locating useful materials in subject disciplines, assisting with format and standards issues, and pro-viding advice on intellectual property issues related to the use of others' materials and the production of new materials.

We can expect to see an increasing number of innovative forms of publication that blend the virtual and the traditional worlds. Recently, the first Blooker Prize for "blooks," which are books based on blogs or websites, was awarded to the author of *Julie & Julia*. This book was the result of blog entries that the author wrote about cooking all of the reci-pes in Julia Child's first volume while living in a small Manhattan apart-ment <www.lulublookerprize.com>. In this case, the success of the digital content prompted the creation of a print product, which has been well received by the public. While this book is not the product of aca-demic research, it is easy to see that the blogs of some academics could result in the production of traditional, printed books that expand on or extend the ideas that they have developed in their blogs. This develop-ment demonstrates another type of creative relationship between print resources and digital resources. Librarians may want to consider how they will preserve selected blogs so that future scholars can study the emergence of phenomena such as "blooks."

DEVELOPING LEARNING OBJECTS

Traditionally, librarians have not been directly involved in curriculum development in the disciplines, other than bibliography courses in the humanities or in encouraging faculty to include information literacy sessions in courses requiring library research projects. In the past, if faculty wrote textbooks, the library's collection would provide underlying resources, but librarians would not get directly involved in the development of the content of the book. Now, as the nature of content in the teaching and learning context is changing, librarians have the opportunity to become more directly involved, as partners with faculty and others, in the creation of curricular materials. They can work closely with instructional technologists, who may work in a different campus unit than the library but who also work closely with faculty. Instructional technologists may be part of a campus center for teaching and learning, part of the information technology operation, or, in some cases, part of the library. They specialize in working with faculty to develop materials or activities for teaching and learning, particularly those including a technology component. In fact, as libraries renovate their facilities and incorporate information or learning commons, frequently offices and work space for the campus center for teaching and learning are included in the information commons space. The mere location of the center in the library does not necessarily produce partnerships between the staffs of the two units. Whether or not they are in the same physical location or administrative unit, librarians should seek out opportunities to learn about the kinds of products the campus teaching and learning center is producing and encourage the incorporation of library materials and information literacy activities into the learning objects produced by the center.

An example of the kinds of products that can be developed by such a center, incorporating library materials, are those from the Columbia University Center for New Media, Teaching and Learning <http://ccnmtl. columbia.edu/web/index.html>, which is administratively part of the library. For example, one of the Center's projects, "Shakespeare and the Book," incorporates digital images of early editions of Shakespeare's works from Special Collections and provides a context for studying authorship, printing, and early performance issues related to Shakespeare's work. Students' learning is enriched through a blending of text and digital image resources, and partnership among faculty, instructional technologists, and librarians can add value to education through these new types of resources. While developing these types of projects is outside of the usual realm of information literacy, such projects help to accomplish overall learning goals related to library resources, and most importantly, encourage student engagement with the primary resources of scholarship. The availability of the digital images does not diminish students' interaction with modern, print copies of Shakespeare; it provides a mechanism for them to easily view multiple items in a convenient spot and minimizes the handling of fragile materials. For students at other universities, the web materials provide a means for easy and open access to rare items that they would not likely easily access on their own campuses. The web images can assist in student engagement with the traditional text, thereby encouraging student learning.

STUDENT-CREATED PROJECTS

There is a concern in some quarters that students have abandoned reading and have been totally seduced by video games and multi-media products. They believe that student work incorporating media is facile and lacking in depth. That view is expressed by a quote in a widely read study that posits that online education has failed: "As most faculty in the US have learned, students have become almost obsessively adroit at 'souping up' their papers, which they submit electronically and which they festoon with charts, animations, and pictures. As one frustrated professor who had just spent a half-hour downloading a student's term paper was heard to remark, 'All I wanted was a simple 20-page paper–what I got looks suspiciously like the outline for a TV show.'"[2] When are student projects "souped up" by non-text elements and when does that content add value? Is a social sciences paper that includes graphs that illustrate points about data unwelcome by traditional faculty? Is an American Studies course project enriched or "dumbed down" by inclusion of images of period costumes, artwork, and the like? Do media-rich student projects generally have less academic merit or imply that students' knowledge is shallower than that of students who produce text-only projects? A closer look at some student-created multi-media projects reveals that they are the products of serious scholarship, built upon the work of standard, scholarly texts. For example, a student at University of Virginia produced a website as a masters project on the film "O Brother Where Art Thou" at University of Virginia.[3] The site includes film and audio clips as well as images, all quite appropriate in studying a film. However, a look at the bibliography of the project reveals that the author relied on many books as background for his research. Alternate media do not negate the need for books; books and other media can complement each other in scholarly work. The use of media in the project was appropriate and helped provide the context for the author's analytical work.

Two students at the University of Southern California (USC) produced a 3-D fly-through simulation of the City of Troy as a student project. The simulation was as detailed, involved, and fast-paced as many commercially available products. Their simulation included finely wrought images of the mythical ancient city. When this author asked the students how they had conceived of the images for their project, whether the images were totally based on their imaginations or on something else, the students replied that they had spent weeks researching their topic at the Getty (Research Library) nearby.[4] Those who would dismiss their product as a "game" to be used merely for entertainment would have missed the important point that the project, as a learning activity, had deeply engaged the student producers and had motivated them to delve deeply into the exploration of their subject.

ENGAGING STUDENT INTERESTS

As librarians think of new ways to engage student interest in books, it is likely that few would think of computer games as a mechanism to use to reach out to students. However, two researchers have found that, "Every time we meet with students, we ask who has checked out a book from the library based on interest generated through game play. Roughly half say yes. In fact, nearly every student we've met who has played *Age of Empires, Civilization, or Rome: Total War* has checked out a book on related topics as a result."[5] Librarians could develop web links, displays in the library, and game nights in the library with an explicit objective of encouraging reading linked to games.

PROMOTING BOOKS AND RESOURCES THROUGH DIGITAL, VISUAL DISPLAYS

Librarians frequently express concern that their users are unaware of the wealth of resources, both print and digital, that are provided by the library. New ways of promoting both print and digital collections can provide a means of exposing the collection to users in creative ways to spark their interest and enthusiasm. For example, Seattle Public Library has an electronic installation, produced by a professor of interactive media at University of California, Santa Barbara, that displays information designed to stimulate community interest in what local people are reading. The display features several panels above the main reference desk that alternately display colorful visualizations of titles of books that have been checked out during the past hour, statistics on the number of books and media that patrons have checked out, titles divided into Dewey classifications, and a "keyword map" that displays terms for items that patrons have checked out.[6] The display is eye-catching and causes library users to pause out of curiosity and view the stream of information passing along the display screens. It quickly becomes obvious that the information is related to library holdings, and the visitor is able to understand, in just a few minutes, some of the rich resources held by the library.

The University of California, Merced is installing large screens on the main floor of its new library onto which they will project digital images of materials from Special Collections and information about the library.[7] They will enable the library to literally show users the rich resources available through the library's systems.

Both of these display mechanisms use digital environments to promote print collections. They demonstrate creative and innovative juxtaposition of the print and digital environments.

PROMOTING COMMUNITY

Libraries can plan and implement community activities that promote reading, directly or indirectly, and that leverage the use of digital and print resources. For example, the University of Minnesota library runs a campus blog service <http://blog.lib.umn.edu/> which promotes a sense of community. Library staff provide advice on ways to incorporate blogs into student learning experiences and occasionally sponsor on-campus, community-building events such as bringing famous bloggers to campus to speak.

Another opportunity for libraries to promote reading are "One Book" programs, where all incoming freshmen read the same book and then campus activities and discussions are planned around it. Public libraries often take the lead in such programs for local communities, but the programs in higher education are frequently administered through orientation or freshman year offices and in many cases are not linked to the library. However, at Michigan State University, the One Book program partnership <http://www.onebook.msu.edu/>, which includes the neighboring city, includes a role for the library–it hosts related events, in one instance screening a film on a topic related to the book.

In the tradition of the "read more about it" program where television viewers were encouraged to visit their local libraries to find resources related to major Public Broadcasting Service programs, libraries can add value to institutionally-related digital collections that are being developed in higher education. For example, the University of California recently announced that it will put a major collection of its educational videos online; it would be a great idea for the affiliated libraries to add "read more about it" web pages to the educational videos. Other institutions will have their own unique opportunities to link faculty or university-produced digital collections to the library's resources.

These types of programs help to make the library a center for both intellectual activity and social communication on academic subjects. By using the digital environment to promote activities and to provide a venue for communication, and then coupling the digital presence with in-person events and print resources, the library can help enrich the informal aspects of the academic experience for its community members.

CONCLUSION

Digital resources and print resources do not have to reside in separate worlds. Libraries can benefit by promoting the synergies between print collections and Internet-based content, products, and services. They can gain more visibility for their collections, enrich the academic experience of students, and provide support for the creativity of the faculty. As the nature of the products of scholarship change, as more and more rich multimedia resources are produced, and as the information environment becomes more crowded with content, libraries and librarians can distinguish themselves by encouraging new kinds of creative connections between print and digital worlds and by providing collections, physical environments, and knowledgeable staff to allow for the creation of new scholarship.

NOTES

1. Koman, Richard. "Remixing Culture: An Interview with Lawrence Lessig." O'Reilly PolicyDev Center, February 24, 2005 <http://www.oreillynet.com/pub/a/policy/2005/02/24/lessig.html>.

2. Zemsky, Robert and William F. Massy. *Thwarted Innovation: What Happened to e-learning and Why.* University of Pennsylvania: The Learning Alliance, 2004, p. 57 <http://www.irhe.upenn.edu/Docs/Jun2004/ThwartedInnovation.pdf>.

3. Cline, John. American Myth Today: *O Brother Where Art Thou?* and the Language of Mythic Space. University of Virginia Master's Program in American Studies <http://xroads.virginia.edu/~ma05/cline/obrother/free6/obrother1.htm>.

4. The students gave their presentation at "Information Commons: Learning Space Beyond the Classroom." Leavey Library 2004 Conference. University of Southern California, September 16-17, 2004 <http://www.usc.edu/isd/libraries/locations/leavey/news/conference/about/> but there is no record of it on the conference website.

5. Squire, Kurt and Constance Steinkuehler. "Meet the Gamers." *Library Journal.* April 15, 2005.

6. "New Data-driven Artwork Installed at Central Library." Seattle Public Library News Release. September 12, 2005 <http://www.spl.org/default.asp?pageID=about_news_detail&cid=1126554289343>.

7. Carlson, Scott. "The Birth of a Research University: Shelve Under 'E' for Electronic." *Chronicle of Higher Education*, April 1, 2005 <http://chronicle.com/weekly/v51/i30/30a02401.htm>.

doi:10.1300/J111v46n02_03

Shaping Our Space:
Envisioning the New Research Library

Joseph J. Branin

SUMMARY. Academic librarians are designing new spaces in their libraries, in some cases through the re-design and renovation of existing facilities, and in rarer cases, through the opportunity to design an entirely new building. At the Ohio State University, the hundred year old, central research library on campus is undergoing a major, $100 million transformation that involves elements of restoration, gutting, tear down, and new building. What are the architectural and library programmatic directions that are guiding this project and other space design projects in research libraries today? How much space should be devoted to print collections and services, and how much space should be devoted to digital services, information commons, and other new demands on library space? The answers are to be found through an exploration of emerging library practices of "content management" and "learning space design" that must be linked to the aesthetics and functionality of effective architecture. doi:10.1300/J111v46n02_04 *[Article copies available for a fee from The Haworth Document Delivery Service: 1-800-HAWORTH. E-mail address: <docdelivery@haworthpress.com> Website: <http://www.HaworthPress.com> © 2007 by The Haworth Press, Inc. All rights reserved.]*

Joseph J. Branin is Director of Libraries, Ohio State University, Columbus, OH (E-mail: branin.1@osu.edu).

[Haworth co-indexing entry note]: "Shaping Our Space: Envisioning the New Research Library." Branin, Joseph J. Co-published simultaneously in *Journal of Library Administration* (The Haworth Information Press, an imprint of The Haworth Press, Inc.) Vol. 46, No. 2, 2007, pp. 27-53; and: *Print vs. Digital: The Future of Coexistence* (ed: Sul H. Lee) The Haworth Information Press, an imprint of The Haworth Press, Inc., 2007, pp. 27-53. Single or multiple copies of this article are available for a fee from The Haworth Document Delivery Service [1-800-HAWORTH, 9:00 a.m. - 5:00 p.m. (EST). E-mail address: docdelivery@haworthpress.com].

Available online at http://jla.haworthpress.com
© 2007 by The Haworth Press, Inc. All rights reserved.
doi:10.1300/J111v46n02_04

27

KEYWORDS. Library space design, library architecture, library facility renovation, collection storage, learning space in libraries, knowledge management, content management, information technology in libraries, the Ohio State University Libraries, William Oxley Thompson Library at Ohio State University

CONTEXT:
THE WILLIAM OXLEY THOMPSON MEMORIAL LIBRARY AT THE OHIO STATE UNIVERSITY

The Ohio State University (OSU) has the 18th largest collection volume count among research libraries in North America.[1] With a print collection approaching six million volumes, a significant online information service, and a total staff of 405, this large, public, research library system serves a population of 50,000 students and 27,000 faculty and staff. The physical plant of the library system is moderately decentralized for a large research library, with twenty facilities on the main campus and six regional campus libraries in the central region of the State. On the main campus in Columbus, Ohio, the library facilities range greatly in age and size, from the historic Orton Hall Library built in 1893 now housing a geology collection of 97,000 volumes (Figure 1), to a twelve year old consolidated Physical Sciences and Engineering Library of 385,000 volumes that is open seven days a week, twenty-four hours a day (Figure 2), to a brand new, design award-winning Architecture Library of 45,000 volumes[2] (Figure 3).

There is also a high-density book storage facility on the edge of campus that houses approximately three million less-frequently used items from the Libraries' collections. This facility, which is open seven days a week with three delivery services a day to central campus library facilities, is modular in design and has two storage modules in operation and almost full to capacity, but with potential for three more modules to be built, each capable of holding about 1.5 million volumes (Figure 4).

At the very center of the University's Columbus campus is the William Oxley Thompson Memorial Library, more simply called the "Main Library" or the "Thompson Library" (Figures 5 and 6).

It is the largest single library in the OSU system by facility size, housing humanities collections and several special collections along with the preservation and central public, technical, and administrative services units of the library system. The Thompson Library provides accommodations for approximately two million volumes of collection, one hundred

FIGURE 1. Orton Hall at Ohio State University

Used with permission.

FIGURE 2. Science and Engineering Library at Ohio State University

Used with permission.

and seventy-five staff, and nine hundred user seats. The facility was built over the last century in three phases from east to west: the original building opened in 1913 (Figure 7), the central book stack tower in 1952 (Figure 8), and the western addition in 1977 (Figure 9). All told, the building has about three hundred thousand gross square feet of space.

FIGURE 3. Knowlton School of Architecture at Ohio State University

Used with permission.

FIGURE 4. Book Depository at Ohio State University

Used with permission.

While serving many generations of students and faculty well and becoming over the last century a familiar landmark building on campus,
the Thompson Library started to draw criticism from users in the
1980s and 1990s for its inadequate space, convoluted design, and declining infrastructure, furnishings, and upkeep. A clear example of

FIGURE 5. Thompson Library on the Ohio State University Oval

Used with permission.

FIGURE 6. William Oxley Thompson Memorial Library at Ohio State University

Used with permission.

FIGURE 7. Thompson Library, Original Building, 1910-1913, Allen & Collins Architects

Used with permission.

this decline can be seen in the before and after images of the Thompson Library's East Reading Room. The most inspiring interior space in the original 1913 building, the east reading room was two stories high with a vaulted ceiling, oak bookcases and tables, and windows overlooking the campus's bucolic Oval (Figure 10). A student describing the East Reading Room (referred to as the "Reference Hall") in its first year of operation in 1913 wrote in the *Ohio State University Monthly*:

> *To return to school one rainy morning and enter the white corridor all alight with soft radiance, to mount the broad main stair was in itself an experience unreal. Then at length to see the quiet grandeur of the vast Reference Hall, high windows to the east, chaste whiteness of the walls, and the high curve of vaulted arches overhead–this was the climax of impressiveness.*[3]

In 1965 this beautiful room was subdivided horizontally to create two one-story reading rooms with more floor space devoted to book stacks.

FIGURE 8. First Addition to Thompson Library, Stack Tower and Two Wings, 1948-1952, Howard Dwight Smith, University Architect

Used with permission.

FIGURE 9. Second Addition to Thompson Library, 1975-1977, Lorenz, Williams, Lively and Likens Architects

Used with permission.

FIGURE 10. East Reading Room at Ohio State University, 1913

Used with permission.

Unfortunately the east reading rooms lost all their charm to clutter and overcrowding (Figure 11).

This example, by the way, points to an all too common problem in research libraries in the second half of the twentieth century that Scott Bennett identified in his study *Libraries Designed for Learning.* According to Bennett, "Library after library has sacrificed reader accommodations to the imperatives of shelving. The crowding out of readers by reading material is one of the most common and disturbing ironies in library space planning."[4] This was certainly the case in the Thompson Library at Ohio State.

By the late 1990s the facility situation in Thompson Library was becoming intolerable. In 1998 a University faculty committee issued a scathing report calling for a general and massive overall of the Thompson Library facility.[5] With a new University President and a new University Librarian coming onboard shortly after the report, the renovation of the Thompson Library became a real University priority in 2000, appropriately at the beginning of the 21st century. As the new

FIGURE 11. East Reading Room, Upper Level, at Ohio State University, post 1965

Used with permission.

University President, Brit Kirwan, stated in his memoir of his Ohio State University years,

> *When I arrived at Ohio State [in 1998], I saw an impressive library structure and visited it. I was positively stunned by how depressing and dilapidated and unimpressive a place it was, so incompatible with our aspirations. You can stand at the library and look at the renovated football stadium and new basketball arena. I asked myself, how can I be part of a university where this happens? For substantive and symbolic reasons, we had to act, and I told the senate that I would consider it a failure if when I leave, we haven't developed the funding for the library renovation.*[6]

Planning for the major renovation of the Thompson Library began in earnest in 2000. First there was a two-year feasibility study conducted by the architectural firms of Shepley Bulfinch Richardson and Abbot and URS Corporation. After reviewing the feasibility options, the University decided on an ambitious plan costing $100 million, with $70 million coming from State capital funds and $30 million from private fund raising. A three-year design phase came next, lead by the architectural firms of Gund Partnership and Acock Associates. It was during this phase that the University decided to stay within the basic footprint of the existing building, keeping the 1913 original building and the 1952 book stacks tower, but removing the eastern wings added in 1952, and tearing down the 1977 second addition and rebuilding this section with a new western front. Total space for the building would remain almost the same, with renovated building growing by only 8,000 square feet to 308,000 gross square feet. Also, the project would follow a one-phase construction strategy, meaning the building would be completely vacated and given over to construction during the actual rebuilding period scheduled for 2006 to 2009.

Throughout the feasibility study and the design phase, librarians at the University, as well as many administrators, faculty, and students, worked closely with the project architects particularly on programmatic issues. How were research libraries changing? How would the use of space in the renovated building affect other libraries and other units on campus? What did users of the library want in their re-made library? Was this an opportunity to reorganize collections and services of the entire library system? How was new information technology affecting the use of space in libraries? How best to answer these questions for the Thompson Library Renovation project, or for any other significant library space design project, occupies the rest of this paper.

CHALLENGE:
BUILDING OR REBUILDING A RESEARCH LIBRARY IN A CHANGING TECHNOLOGY AND HIGHER EDUCATION ENVIRONMENT

In any library space design project today, certain basic challenges must be faced and met. These include:

1. financial challenges,
2. architectural design challenges,

3. the impact of changing information technology on library services and space needs,
4. multiple constituents' differing library needs and perceptions of what the "library" should be, and
5. the effect of new learning and research patterns at the University on library services and space.

Although all these challenges can be difficult and complex, the more factual or explicit ones, such as financial and architectural challenges, tend to be easier to uncover and express, if not overcome. New buildings, renovations, or remodelings are often constrained or partly defined by the site, by the existing architecture, and certainly by the level of funding available. The budget and architecture for a project should, of course, respond to the more tacit programmatic challenges of information technology demands and user needs, but in the end, dollars, real estate, steel, and concrete do put hard and limiting definitions on any space design project.

For librarians, the tacit programmatic challenges in library space design are the most interesting and most important. Architects, contractors, and funders want to know what to build and how much it will cost, and they should ask librarians to answer these question by having them describe what a 21st century library and its spaces should look like now and into the foreseeable future. However, the tacit programmatic answers are usually not as clear and straight forward as are the answers to the explicit financial and architectural questions. For example, ask constituents of the research library–students, faculty, alumni–what they think the library should be, and you are likely to get multiple and conflicting answers today. In the Thompson Library Renovation project, all constituent groups were involved from the beginning, participating in surveys, focus groups, town meetings, and individual sessions during the feasibility study and the design phase. Here are some representative examples of their opinions and recommendations:

- *Books (again, things you can hold in your hands, not a text that is one click away) are highly underrated in our society . . . Our society's rampant and depressing anti-intellectualism . . . Save the books please.*–Graduate student, 2004.
- *Actually it has been years since I needed a physical library. I check out books on-line and they come to my office. I download*

journal articles over the Internet. My main reason for visiting the library now is to visit the coffee shop.–Faculty member, 2004.

- *Keep the stacks.*–Alumnus, 2003.
- *Get rid of the stacks–it is one of the creepiest places I have ever been.*–Anonymous, 2003.
- *There should be group study rooms. I often need to work with my classmates in group projects.*–Undergraduate, 2002.
- *As graduate students spend a large part of their time in the library, it is only fair that they have access to quiet, accessible work spaces.*–Graduate student, 2003.
- *Why can't you just leave the library alone? All anyone at OSU cares about anymore is 'Preparing for the future! Making things modern!' If I would have known that my four years at OSU would have been nothing but construction sites around campus, I would have chosen another university.*–Undergraduate, 2004.[7]

Clearly there is not consensus among constituents about the future of the research library. The library today is in a state of transition, largely brought on by the rapid advance of networked digital information technology. In a transition period, constituents, as well as librarians, are often inconsistent and confused about future directions. OCLC's recent study *Perceptions of Libraries and Information Resources* points this out very well. While students and the general public are turning increasingly to networked digital information services for their information needs, these same constituents still associate "library" with "books" and have what might be called an "nostalgic" perception of the library. According to Cathy De Rosa, one of the principal contributors to the OCLC report, *"Libraries' mindshare in this new self-service e-resource environment is also clear: behind the newer entrants. Libraries' continued importance as trusted information provider is evident and, overall, users have positive, if outdated, views of the 'Library.' "*[8] I heard a similar view expressed by a library director who designed and opened a new research library in the 1990s. When asked for his advice about getting faculty involvement in design planning, the director's comment was that it is critical to get such input but I should keep in mind that faculty are likely to design the library they fondly remember using as graduate students several decades in the past.

ENVISIONING:
THE BEST SPACE AND PROGRAMMATIC LIBRARY DESIGN
FOR TODAY'S AND TOMORROW'S STUDENTS
AND FACULTY

How do librarians make sense of this confusing and sometimes contradictory input from user constituencies about the 21st century library? After several years of intensive study that involved considerable constituent input, usage trend data, professional reading, travel to see new library space, and discussions with library consultants and architects, the Thompson Library Renovation project staff gradually found and settled on two basic programmatic themes that helped organize and give meaning to all the information and design ideas they were gathering. These two basic themes were:

1. new practices in collection and content management, and
2. creating a "learning" organization and "learning" spaces in the library.

These two themes lead us to interesting programmatic reorganization and redeployment of collections, services, and staff in the Thompson Library and in the whole library system, and they helped us inform the work of our architects in designing space that we think is beautiful, functional, and flexible for today's and tomorrow's academic library user.

NEW PRACTICES
IN COLLECTION AND CONTENT MANAGEMENT

The "collection" has been a defining element of a research library program. In several earlier articles I have described in some detail the changing nature of collection's work in the research library, arguing that we must see this element of our responsibility as having evolved from collection development, to collection management, to what today should be, knowledge or content management.[9] For the purposes of this paper, I will limit my remarks to some of the elements of knowledge or content management that are most directly affecting space design issues today.

It is really only now, at the beginning of the 21st century, that research librarians can look at multiple motivations for building new space or redesigning old library space. Because until only recently, accommodating growing print collections was what research library facilities were pretty much single-mindedly about. Today that situation is changing with new storage options for print material, consortial collection building, and the new demands on librarians for digital content management and services.

Certainly print as a medium for scholarship has not gone away, and doesn't appear to be going away in the near future. Large research libraries in the Association of Research Libraries have steadily added a hundred thousand or more new print volumes to their collections each year.[10] What is changing is how these print volumes are stored and shared. By 2000, the Thompson Library facility at Ohio State, like many other central research library facilities, was overcrowded with book stacks, and the stacks themselves were overcrowded with too many volumes. The Thompson Library was estimated at its peak of overcrowding to hold more than two and half million print volumes, but at the expense of reader seating and proper preservation shelving (Figure 12).

The OSU library system has been fortunate to be part of the OhioLINK consortium. One important component of this state-wide library cooperative is a system of five regional library depository facilities, where lesser used material can be stored and serviced efficiently in high density, preservation quality space. One of these depositories is located in central Ohio on the edge of the OSU campus and managed by the OSU Libraries (see Figure 1). Module two of the central Ohio book depository came on line in 2002 (Figure 13), and the OSU librarians began an aggressive program of transferring appropriate material from its central campus libraries, particularly from the Thompson Library, to the book depository.

Over the last decade, the collection size in the Thompson Library has been reduced from over two million volumes to approximately one and half million volumes. This transfer of collections, which became more aggressive in the last four years, was done to prepare for the renovation of the Thompson Library, but for other important reasons as well: to create more reader and information technology service space in the central campus libraries and to better preserve collections through better

FIGURE 12. Book Stacks in Thompson Library, 2001

Used with permission.

FIGURE 13. High Density, Preservation Storage in the Book Depository

Used with permission.

storage. Overcrowding does not serve collections or users well. The book depository program gives collection managers the useful option of keeping core, frequently-used collections close to users in proper storage space configurations in central campus library facilities, while storing lesser-used material more efficiently off campus but serviceably through the online catalog and quick document delivery service. The book depository option played a critical role in our space allocation decisions for collection storage, helping us create a proper balance with other programmatic needs in the new design of the Thompson Library.

Consortial arrangements and effective document delivery services, along with new storage options, have become key factors in content management at Ohio State both for print and digital collections. Everything does not have to be physically in a campus library or in an institution's book depository anymore to be part of one's collection, although this is still a controversial view for some constituents and librarians. For academic libraries in Ohio, OhioLINK enables its eighty-eight members to share a common library automation and request system, making discovery, request, and delivery of print material from any of its locations simple, quick, and inexpensive. Patrons do direct requests, and resource sharing has steadily increased since 1994 (Figure 14).[11]

Because resource sharing among OhioLINK libraries is made so easy and quick, all types of constituents participate, even undergraduates who often need library material at the last minute. Undergraduates account for almost 40% of the borrowing through OhioLINK (Figure 15).

Resource sharing is really an essential component of the content management program at Ohio State University. Our own commitment to library cooperation in collection management combined with our membership in OhioLINK makes us a standout among the Association of Research Libraries when it comes to resource sharing, with our lending and borrowing statistics much above the average ARL transaction level (Figure 16).

With a new emphasis on knowledge or content management, the OSU Libraries has expanded its responsibilities to collect and preserve more types and formats of academic information. The Libraries has a digital repository program called the Knowledge Bank and is currently working on a faculty expertise system called OSU Pro.[12] The space implications for a knowledge management program include, in our case, more space to house partnership organizations, more office space for in-

FIGURE 14. OhioLINK Patron Borrowing, 1994-2003

Filled Online Patron Borrowing Requests

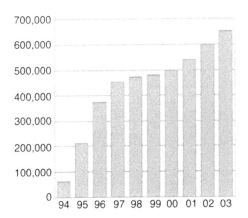

FIGURE 15. OhioLINK Borrowing by Patron Type, 1994-2003

Online Patron Borrowing by Patron Type

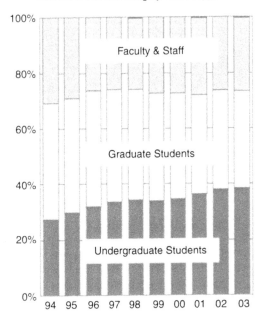

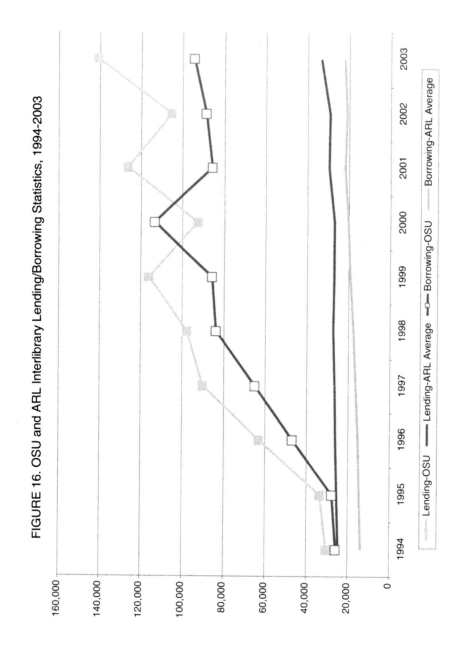

FIGURE 16. OSU and ARL Interlibrary Lending/Borrowing Statistics, 1994-2003

44

formation technology staff, more information technology rich public learning spaces, and a more robust power and data infrastructure throughout our facilities. In the renovation of the Thompson Library, for example, we decided to bring the senior administrations of both the University Libraries and the Chief Information Officer together in a common office suite in this facility, since we do so much work together on knowledge and content management services.

CREATING A LEARNING ORGANIZATION AND NEW LEARNING SPACES

Managing our collections and more types of content in new ways and integrating these information resources with new space design opportunities allows us to create some exciting learning spaces in our library facilities. By limiting the size and growth of print collection storage in our campus libraries, we have more space for the amount and variety of public seating, services, and programs offered in our facilities around the core information resources that remain. In the renovated Thompson Library, for instance, there will be more space, front and center, for special collections services, better user and browsing space in the open stacks, and more opportunities for exhibits, displays, lectures, and seminars that make good use of the Libraries' print and digital resources. Already our design planning for the Thompson Library has led us to consider and offer more programs in our facilities that support learning and attract more students and faculty to library resources and services. We have in the last few years added a café to the library and initiated a leisure reading collection, a weekly read aloud program, a large-course textbook open reserve, displays of student research projects, more student education programs, more academic lectures, and an expanded document delivery program called Article Express.[13]

All this is really part of an attempt to create more responsive learning space and programs in our library facilities. In our planning and design work for the Thompson Library Renovation, we were very influenced by the recent work of Scott Bennet on library space design. We found his study *Libraries Designed for Learning* extremely helpful, and we came to use him as a library consultant to our renovation project. Bennet's basic contention is that in the 1990s library space design tended to look back rather than forward. Bennet observes that while in the 1990s "higher education saw transformative changes in student learning, faculty teaching methods, and information technology," library space designs "were not fundamentally different in concept from those designed in the 1960s."[14] Certainly information technology has changed, and while one may question how "transformational" teaching and learning in higher education really has been in the last twenty years, there are at least signs of and more experimentation with new active learning processes by faculty and students.

In our space design planning at Ohio State, we rallied around three activities in creating new learning space. First, we came to place a greater emphasis on more space for and more attention to the social learning needs of students. This meant a café in the library, better amenities and upkeep, more exhibit and display space for student use, much more collaborative spaces for group work, but also the need for traditional quiet study spaces. For our particular renovation project in Thompson Library, we are doubling the number of user seats in the facility, going from about one to two thousand seats, and we are reducing the overall amount of space allocated to collection storage.

Second, we were attracted to the wave of Information or Learning Commons being created in academic libraries in the last five years. These information commons are technology rich, often with one-stop help for reference or technology assistance that is managed as a partnership between the library and information technology units on campus. Our project team visited a good number of these new Information Commons, and we were most impressed with the installation at Georgia Institute of Technology Library in Atlanta.[15] At Georgia Tech we found an Information Commons that had become a real and very popular center for learning activity outside the classroom at that University. With a rich array of productivity and multimedia software, the Commons at Georgia Tech receives heavy use during its 24 × 7 schedule. Most importantly, I think, for its success as a real learning space, is its true partnership of library and information technology staff with well trained and motivated student assistant help.

And third and finally, we rallied around developing library staff commitment to learning as a key value in our organization. We created a library working group, the OSU Libraries Learning Group, to look at how best we should deploy our staff and space for learning in the future.[16] This task force issued a very influential report in 2004 that among other things recommended:

- Setting learning as a priority in the Libraries: learning over service approaches.
- Experimentation in use of space: design decisions be made in ways that maximize possibilities for future change.
- Collaboration with other campus agencies.
- Bringing students, faculty, and librarians together in the library: shift in behavior toward welcoming contact with students in the library.

After five years of intense and serious space design planning, I can look back now and summarize the concepts and programmatic thrusts that I think most influenced or gave meaning to our work. The following five concepts helped us work with our constituents, funders, and architects to design library space that we hope will be beautiful, functional, flexible, and higher responsive to the needs of students and faculty in the 21st century.

1. An emphasis on content management, learning, and outreach responsibilities of research librarians, staff, and student assistants: new assignments and accountability, redeployment of personnel, more collaborative team efforts.
2. Consolidation of collections and service points: in our Thompson Library Project we are consolidating humanities and social sciences collections, a number of special collections areas, and consolidating and reducing the number of reference and circulation service points.
3. More collaboration with other libraries and other campus agencies.
4. Primacy of public space in library facilities that is varied, flexible, and information technology rich.
5. Creating flexible "learning space" that brings students, faculty, librarians, and information resources and services together for active learning.

LIBRARY ARCHITECTURE FOR BEAUTIFUL, FUNCTIONAL, AND FLEXIBLE SPACE

I will end as it should end with the architecture itself, in this case the architectural plans for the transformed William Oxley Thompson Memorial Library. After more than five years of planning and design, the remaking of the central library at Ohio State Universtiy is about to begin. Reconstruction will take three years, and during that time period the building will be completely vacated with all collections, staff, and services relocated to other facilities on campus. (The logistics of a one-phase, massive library renovation project are for another story to tell.) In 2009, I believe we will move back into a truly beautiful, functional, and flexible research library for the 21st century. The eastern façade of the building will retain and improve its original Renaissance Revival style (Figure 17). Two small wings added in the 1950s will be removed, and windows will be added and enlarged on the original building and stacks tower.

The western façade of the building will change dramatically (Figure 18). The 1977 addition to the west of the stacks tower will be torn down, and a new, more complementary addition will be built. The new western façade will present a second "front" for the facility, pedestrian friendly, with a new entrance from the west, a new café, and a dramatic reading room and roof garden on this side of the building.

Two atria with large sky lights will be constructed on either side of the central stacks tower, and the first six levels of the stacks tower will be open to the atria, creating a much more unified, open, and light filled building (Figures 19 and 20).

The stacks tower will house open, general collections in the humanities and social sciences and below ground will be compact closed stack storage for special collections material. The first five levels of the building will house special collections services, general library services, visible and easy to find staff offices, and a great variety of public spaces that will include information commons, quiet reading areas, group and instruction rooms, and expanded exhibit and display space. Finally, there will be three special, inspiring reading rooms in the library: the resorted, traditional East Reading Room (Figure 21), a contemporary West Reading Room (Figure 22) in the new west addition, and a spectacular Tower Reading Room at the top of the stacks tower (Figure 23).

FIGURE 17. Eastern Façade of the Renovated Thompson Library

Used with permission.

FIGURE 18. Western Façade of the Renovated Thompson Library

Used with permission.

FIGURE 19. Cross-Section of the Renovated Thompson Library

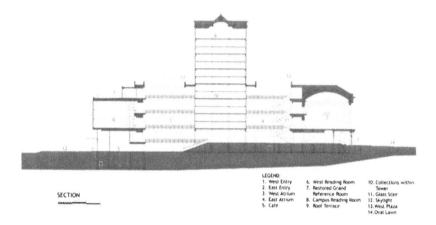

SECTION

LEGEND:
1. West Entry
2. East Entry
3. West Atrium
4. East Atrium
5. Cafe
6. West Reading Room
7. Restored Grand
   Reference Room
8. Campus Reading Room
9. Roof Terrace
10. Collections within
    Tower
11. Glass Stair
12. Skylight
13. West Plaza
14. Oval Lawn

Used with permission.

FIGURE 20. Atrium Space in the Renovated Thompson Library

Used with permission.

FIGURE 21. East Reading Room in the Renovated Thompson Library

Used with permission.

FIGURE 22. West Reading Room in the Renovated Thompson Library

Used with permission.

FIGURE 23. Tower Reading Room in the Renovated Thompson Library

Used with permission.

NOTES

1. Association of Research Libraries, *ARL Statistics 2003-2004*. Washington, DC: Association of Research Libraries, 2005, p. 70.

2. The Ohio State University's new Knowlton School of Architecture Library received the Award of Excellence in the American Institute of Architects and the American Library Association's 2005 Library Building Award Program.

3. Charles St. John Chubb, "Architecture and the New Library," *Ohio State University Monthly*, vol. 4, no. 6, February 1913, pp. 5-8.

4. Scott Benett, *Libraries Designed for Learning*, Washington DC: Council on Library and Information Resources, 2003, p. 5.

5. Ohio State University, *Library Task Force Report*, June 9, 1998.

6. Chris Perry, *The Kirwan Years, 1998-2002*, Columbus, Ohio: The Ohio State University Press, 2006, p. 81.

7. User comments gathered over a five-year period, 2000 to 2005, as part of The Ohio State University Thompson Library Renovation Project.

8. OCLC Online Computer Library Center, *Perceptions of Libraries and Information Resources*, Dublin, Ohio: OCLC, 2005, p. ix.

9. Joseph J. Branin, "Knowledge Management in Academic Libraries: Building the Knowledge Bank at the Ohio State University," *Journal of Library Administration*, Vol. 39, No.4, 2003, pp. 41-56. See also Joseph J. Branin, France Groen, and Suzanne Thorin, "The Changing Nature of Collection Management in Research Libraries," *Library Resources & Technical Services* 44, January 2000, pp. 23-33.

10. *ARL Statistics 2003-2004*, p. 71.

11. OhioLINK Ohio Library and Information Network, *Snapshot 2005: Connecting Ohio Higher Education to the World of Information*, Columbus, Ohio: OhioLINK, 2005.

12. The Ohio State University Libraries' Knowledge Bank <https://kb.osu.edu/dspace/index.jsp> and OSU Pro <https://pro.osu.edu/>.

13. The Ohio State University Libraries' Article Express <https://www.illiad.osu.edu/illiad/osu/ArticleExpressLogon.html>.

14. Scott Bennet, *Libraries Designed for Learning*, p. 2.

15. Georgia Institute of Technology, Library and Information Center, Library West Commons <http://www.atlantahighered.org/members/git_library.asp> Tech Information Commons.

16. Scott Bennet, *Report of the OSU Libraries Learning Group*, Columbus, Ohio: The Ohio State University Libraries, 2004 <https://kb.osu.edu/dspace/handle/1811/202>.

doi:10.1300/J111v46n02_04

JSTOR:
Past, Present, and Future

Michael P. Spinella

SUMMARY. JSTOR has become a standard offering at most U.S. universities and colleges, as well as a growing number of higher education institutions outside the U.S. This paper will track the growth of JSTOR since its inception in 1995 as an experimental digitization project to today as an archive of over 500 scholarly titles in 40 disciplines. We will consider the two threads of JSTOR's mission—to safeguard titles in a digital form, and to provide access to them as broadly as possible—and assess the value the project has provided to the academic community. In addition, there will be some discussion of future directions and challenges for JSTOR. doi:10.1300/J111v46n02_05 *[Article copies available for a fee from The Haworth Document Delivery Service: 1-800-HAWORTH. E-mail address: <docdelivery@haworthpress.com> Website: <http://www.HaworthPress.com> © 2007 by The Haworth Press, Inc. All rights reserved.]*

KEYWORDS. JSTOR, library participation in, scholarly publications, preservation, JSTOR usage, JSTOR costs, digitization, library space utilization, JSTOR mission

Michael P. Spinella is Executive Director, JSTOR New York, 149 Fifth Avenue, 8th Floor, New York, NY 10010 (E-mail: mspinella@jstar.org).

The author wishes to acknowledge the substantial contributions to this paper made by colleagues at JSTOR and Ithaka, particularly Heidi McGregor, Sherry Aschenbrenner, John Kiplinger, Kimberly Lutz, Stephanie Krueger, and Kevin Guthrie.

[Haworth co-indexing entry note]: "JSTOR: Past, Present, and Future." Spinella, Michael P. Co-published simultaneously in *Journal of Library Administration* (The Haworth Information Press, an imprint of The Haworth Press, Inc.) Vol. 46, No. 2, 2007, pp. 55-78; and: *Print vs. Digital: The Future of Coexistence* (ed: Sul H. Lee) The Haworth Information Press, an imprint of The Haworth Press, Inc., 2007, pp. 55-78. Single or multiple copies of this article are available for a fee from The Haworth Document Delivery Service [1-800-HAWORTH, 9:00 a.m. - 5:00 p.m. (EST). E-mail address: docdelivery@haworthpress.com].

doi:10.1300/J111v46n02_05

INTRODUCTION

For the past decade, JSTOR has been steadfastly committed to two goals–preserving scholarly journals in electronic form and providing access to them as widely as possible. In this paper, I want to share my own assessment of the progress we have been able to make toward these aims as well as the considerable distance that we have yet to traverse. I also want to observe how various realities have evolved from those that characterized the scholarly communications environment in 1995, when JSTOR was conceived, and to ponder some of the implications of these transitions.

When I say "we" in the context of accomplishments and work yet to be done, I have in mind the dedicated staff at JSTOR as well as the libraries, publishers, foundations, trustees, and researchers who have contributed to and supported the project. JSTOR exists at a nexus of cooperation among communities–and we are ever mindful of the need to nurture and cultivate that cooperative spirit. It is neither accidental nor inevitable, so one of my themes today will be to suggest the importance and value of a collaborative approach, even among communities and institutions where a certain amount of tension is unavoidable and may be productive.

In reflecting on JSTOR over the past decade, I am reminded of a lesson noted by Hal Varian in the foreword to Roger Schonfeld's book, *JSTOR: A History*, that chronicles JSTOR's early development. He said, "Be flexible." In many ways, as our efforts have evolved over time, we have tried to follow this sage advice, but flexibility requires discipline and care, and it becomes more challenging as young projects mature. JSTOR's mission is perhaps much broader than many may realize. Succinctly stated we exist to help the academic community take advantage of new technologies to facilitate education and research. JSTOR's own evolution as it strives to fulfill these ambitious aims signals this need for flexibility, but perhaps the clearest example is the emergence of our new sister organization, Portico. Portico launched last year, after almost 3 years in development, first as an initiative within JSTOR, then as an incubated project of Ithaka. JSTOR continues its close affiliation with Portico and has provided part of the start-up funds required. The purpose of the new organization is to provide a solution to the growing and unsettled problem of how to archive born-digital content. I will have occasion to refer to Portico in other sections of this talk. For now, I merely want to introduce it, and note that Portico takes a very different approach to its business model than JSTOR. It was developed expressly to advance JSTOR's broad mission, recognizing that community needs and the opportunities to respond to preservation of electronic content should be met in a new way.

It may seem a gross understatement to say that quite a lot has changed in a decade. In 1995, the process of digitization was expensive and lacked standardization. The value of bringing legacy content online was unclear; most publishers viewed their back content as liabilities rather than assets. Indeed there were questions in some disciplines about the merits of putting current issues of journals online at all. Libraries and scholars were also reluctant to give up printed copies. Many preferred the look and feel of print to the glare of a screen, and some felt print conveyed graphics and color reproductions more truly.

Today, digitization is less expensive, is of reasonably good quality, and is occurring on a massive scale. There is very little doubt about the general value of putting both legacy and current content online. Of course, there are still many unanswered questions about the long-term economic viability of such efforts, and what the business model(s) will or should be. We remain in transition, and are working to understand the forces for and against the co-existence of print and electronic resources. As recently as 2001, for example, over 30% of titles participating in JSTOR did not have their current issues online. Today, that number has diminished considerably, but remains at about 15%. Journals in disciplines such as Art History face questions about the viability of online publishing given both limitations of technology and the complex rights issues surrounding images. Certainly not all readers are prepared to forego the beneficial tactile and visual qualities of print, even if they now recognize many other advantages of having content available online. Debate surrounding the serials crisis has also evolved with technological advances, raising new questions about the economics of the creation, distribution, and management of intellectual property. Who owns scholarly literature, and how should it be preserved, delivered, and used online?

At its founding, JSTOR was fundamentally an economic-driven endeavor. It was established to see whether technology could be deployed to save some of the resources that educational institutions find themselves having to invest in building, maintaining, and expanding their libraries. William G. Bowen, who will retire this year as the President of the Mellon Foundation, became interested in the possibilities of digitization of scholarly journals when, in his role as a trustee of Denison University, he learned of the need for a massive, and very costly, library expansion. As the trustees contemplated a capital campaign for library growth, Mr. Bowen wondered if technology could offer a better and more sustainable path.

It quickly became apparent that the goal of saving library shelf space entailed a number of other requirements and responsibilities. The initial concern, of course, was whether digitization of scholarly literature could be accomplished at a sufficient level of quality and economy to be practical. A related but different question had to do with reader preferences–would a digital copy be accepted as an adequate substitute for print? Even if this worked, it was apparent that libraries would not be able to remove printed works from shelves, thereby beginning to realize the potential savings, without assurances that the electronic versions would be complete, secure, and consistently available. This raised the bar–electronic surrogates also had to be persistent and 'portable' to successor technologies. There were practical challenges besides the technology, such as the need to gather and quality check complete runs in print of the titles to be digitized, and the tricky problem of securing rights to the material. It was apparent that for the effort to succeed, it would require a network of cooperation among publishers and librarians, where no such network existed.

JSTOR UPDATE

Although JSTOR started as a straightforward attempt to reduce some of the expense institutions have to bear to house their vast collections of scholarly works, as the core idea was investigated, complex requirements and a broader set of objectives emerged. From this, there are at least four criteria that I consider essential for judging the success and durability of JSTOR:

1. How broad and deep is the community participation in the project?
2. What practices and commitments ensure the persistence and security of the archive?
3. How broadly accessible and useful is the content?
4. Is library participation economical and sustainable?

Assessing our progress involves both objective measures and many subjective judgments. As I discuss the measures of our progress, I will also point out where I think JSTOR still has work to do on each of these fundamental issues. More important, we have come to recognize that the community's objectives and expectations will continue to evolve over time, and so, in a very real sense, our work is never done. In addition, where appropriate, I will point out areas where our experience or challenges seem to have broader implications for the community as we continue to transition toward better online content management and delivery.

Community Participation

The question of the breadth and depth of community participation in JSTOR hinges, of course, on how we define community. JSTOR has from inception aimed to serve the worldwide higher education community, and has sought to balance the interests and needs of librarians, scholars, and publishers. As the archive has grown, the value of access to it has become evident in a number of other education-related communities. We have begun to develop outreach efforts to secondary schools, government agencies, research institutions, and museums. As we seek to broaden JSTOR access to these new communities, we are challenged by Hal Varian's reminder to "be flexible." And flexibility has also been required as we consider new business models and outreach strategies. How well has JSTOR served this diverse community, and how widely is access available?

Figure 1 summarizes our progress mainly in our core higher education community since the first collection was released in 1997. What is pleasing to note here is the steady and vigorous growth of participation among smaller libraries.

JSTOR's international presence has grown more rapidly than any other area in the past few years. In the librarian community, there is a widely shared sense of responsibility for preserving the scholarly record, and, of course, we have long recognized the value to all researchers of enabling scholars to communicate and collaborate across boundaries. Figure 2 illustrates the growth of international participation in recent years compared to new institutional participation in the U.S. As of today, we have reached a point where institutions outside the U.S. represent nearly half of our participation, and we expect that proportion to grow even further in the coming years.

But our international growth has not been distributed equally around the globe. We have made increasingly vigorous efforts to encourage more institutions in developing nations to participate in JSTOR, but this remains in our view a place where we can and should do considerably more. Figure 3 illustrates our participation levels by region, and as you can see there are some big gaps. While we are proud of our progress in

Print vs. Digital: The Future of Coexistence

FIGURE 1. Library Participation by Category

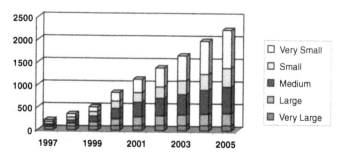

FIGURE 2. International vs. U.S. Percentage Increases

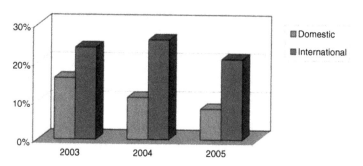

FIGURE 3. JSTOR Participation by Region 2000, 2005

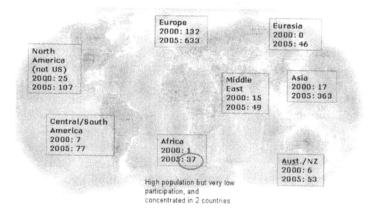

some countries such as China, India, and Pakistan, we are by no means satisfied with the breadth of access in most other developing nations, where we may have only a handful of participating institutions, or indeed, no presence at all. In response to this, our Board of Trustees has recently supported our establishing a new program designed to significantly increase access throughout Africa by waiving fees to institutions there.

Let's turn to other communities to assess progress there. Publisher support of JSTOR has been historically quite strong. Caught between open access pressures and increasing demands from users for more content and tools online, publishers have faced a number of challenges in the past decade. Still, their support for JSTOR has grown and we enjoy strong relationships with many publishers and editors. Today we work with 368 publishers, who have entrusted a total of 758 titles to the archive. We work with publishers across the spectrum from commercial to scholarly societies, to university presses. The next chart, Figure 4, shows the proportions of each, and indicates that JSTOR is most prevalent among society and university publishers.

Just as we have emphasized the importance of international participation from libraries, we also increasingly look to the worldwide community of publishers to contribute journals to the archive. There has been a very high level of interest–in fact, more than we have the capacity to serve–but we are pleased to be making steady progress toward including a broader array of journals from outside the U.S. Table 1 shows the distribution of countries outside the U.S. where JSTOR participating publishers are based.

FIGURE 4. Participating Publishers by Type

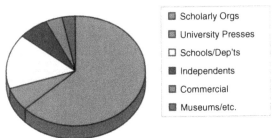

TABLE 1. Participating International Publishers

Country	Publishers
UK	37
Canada	10
France	5
Germany	4
Sweden	4
Netherlands	3
Switzerland	3
Australia, Belgium, Japan	2 each
Argentina, Austria, Croatia, Egypt, Hungary, India, Italy, Mexico, Peru, and Poland	1 each

The table indicates that JSTOR is still a resource largely comprised of English language journals, but with a growing international list of titles. Even among these publishers, most titles are published in English, so clearly this is an area we need to work on more. We have begun, especially in the disciplines of art history, Latin American Studies, music, and religion to archive more non-English titles. Among signed titles, 33 journals have significant French-language content and 22 contain a number of German-language articles. There is a handful of journals with Italian and Spanish content, and we do include, on a more limited basis, some Arabic, Greek, and Chinese articles. Languages such as these which use non-roman characters are a particular technical challenge for us, but this year we are experimenting with journals in Chinese, Japanese, and Korean to see how effectively we can scan and index them.

Since we view publishers as part of the community we serve, we also seek to ensure that they find value in JSTOR participation, just as we look to provide value to libraries and end users. Besides a modest revenue sharing program, JSTOR is working to provide links from the archive to current issues held on the publisher's site. And in 2005, we introduced a content sharing program that enables publishers to obtain a complete copy of their legacy content once we digitize it so that they can integrate it into their own publication services to subscribers.

Beyond publishers and institutions of higher education, we believe JSTOR has a place at every level of the education and research spectrum, not just in universities. Many of the titles archived in JSTOR are useful in secondary schools, research institutions, corporations, and public libraries. We have not approached for-profit entities yet, but in just the last few years, we have begun to introduce JSTOR in secondary schools, museums, public libraries, and more broadly in government agencies throughout the world. We have learned that it is essential to tailor our outreach efforts to the needs of the particular community we are addressing. In many of these communities, for example, we have taken a completely different approach to our pricing model, enabling institutions in these sectors to receive access to all titles in JSTOR for a single fee, instead of dividing it into collections. Still, we have a very long way to go. Our successes so far with secondary schools, public libraries, and museums have been very modest in scope, and almost entirely within the U.S.

Still one more form of participation aimed at increasing access is our work with linking partners and other types of collaborating organizations. We work with major A&I databases, search engines or aggregators in several disciplines to make our data available so that accurate links may be established to content archived in JSTOR. For example, we work with AnthroSource for Anthropology, ABC-CLIO and the History Co-op for History, REPEC for Economics, as well as Cambridge Scientific Abstracts, and most recently have entered into an arrangement enabling Google Scholar to index the archive. Table 2 shows the growing importance of linking from outside resources to the overall usage of content in JSTOR. Since 2001, while the overall number of Articles Viewed has increased more than 7-fold, links into JSTOR have increased by 32 times. Not shown on the chart is a spike in the early part of this year, bringing in around 4 million links in only two months–apparently the result of Google's recently completed index of JSTOR.

TABLE 2. Activity from Linking Partners 2001-2005

	2001	2002	2003	2004	2005
Articles Viewed	7,928,405	14,645,589	25,934,992	35,263,463	59,788,099
Links	207,278	1,453,751	2,952,760	4,728,941	6,990,341
# Links Incorrectly Resolved*	12,328	98,898	317,949	603,925	951,786
Links/Articles Viewed	2.61%	9.93%	11.39%	13.41%	11.69%
% Links Incorrectly Resolved*	5.95%	6.80%	10.77%	12.77%	13.62%

*Refers to links that attempt to locate an article in JSTOR using a non-conforming URL.

Archiving

The first measure of JSTOR's progress on archiving is, of course, the amount of content in the archive. I have already mentioned that there are 758 titles signed from 350 publishers. But not all of these titles have been digitized yet. Currently, the JSTOR archive contains approximately 590 titles, comprising some 20 million pages of scholarly works from as early as 1665. The archive covers important journals in over 40 disciplines.

In order for the academic and publishing communities to take actions based on the availability of this archive, they must have confidence that our decisions will be guided by an overarching commitment to preservation and that the organization is financially sustainable. It is essential for JSTOR to provide our diverse constituents with assurances that electronic versions of print and born-digital content from JSTOR participating publishers will remain safe and accessible online should libraries begin to adopt electronic-only subscriptions, or to discard or remotely store issues. As technology advances, older electronic formats might become obsolete and effectively lost to the community. Our organizational commitment to archiving a title entails a promise to preserve it for the very long term, and a preparedness to convert the files to successor technologies as needed. At this point, we have developed an array of practices that, collectively, cover these most fundamental issues. JSTOR's detailed archiving practices and standards evolve with time, but many aspects have remained stable.

As you may know, when JSTOR accepts a publication for archiving, we commit to retaining the full run of the journal, including all known previous titles. We scan every page of every issue we can acquire, including advertisements, front and back matter, and even blank pages when they are part of a pagination sequence. We investigate each title's history in an effort to be sure of what issues–including special issues that are sometimes unnumbered–and what prior titles have been published. Then we set out to obtain a copy of each issue to be digitized. This is all amazingly detailed and time-consuming work. We keep track of any issues that are missing or had unusable pages so that we can fill them in later when we locate replacements.

JSTOR now supports two paper repositories–one at Harvard and one at the University of California–that will, when complete, contain the full runs of the first 353 titles digitized for the JSTOR archive. This year, we expect to authorize two more partners for 'phase 2' of the repository project. These will cover the remaining titles already in or signed up for the archive, as well as providing us some capacity for future collections. The paper repositories are primarily copies of last resort to be used in the unlikely event we would need to restore all or part of the archive after a catastrophic event. Of course, we maintain multiple copies of the digital archive, both online and off in three locations, to decrease the likelihood of catastrophic loss. We also will occasionally rely on the paper repositories for rescanning when we change our specifications, if the change necessitates going back to the original works.

JSTOR has taken great care to create indexing, or metadata capturing, guidelines for each title we agree to archive. Staff librarians review the past issues of the title in order to document the presence of specific kinds of metadata on the printed page and patterns of formatting and placement for that metadata. Changes and exceptions to the patterns are noted as well so that the digitization vendors have a complete record of the organization of the intellectual content of a journal. We have chosen standards that we believe permit high quality and a reasonable likelihood of convertibility as technology evolves. In addition, we are committed to retroactively upgrading all our digital versions of articles whenever we change our own archiving or digitization standards. One example is an image compositing process we introduced in 2003.

We use a standard in digitizing legacy print content that we call 'faithful replication.' This standard calls for us to recreate on screen as precisely as possible, the look, crispness, and color reproduction quality of the original printed page. It sounds simple enough, but prior to our developing the image compositing process, we had some difficulty meeting the standard of 'faithful replication' when a title uses rich color illustrations along with text on the page. The digitization specifications for producing crisp black and white text are not best for vivid color reproduction, so we had to accept less than perfect color. We resolved the problem initially by placing a thumbnail link to the full color graphic at the bottom of the page, as shown in the 'before' page image at left, but this is less than desirable since it removes the image from its context and may make caption text less than crisp. With image compositing, we are able to meld the best color reproduction together with the best text reproduction onto a single page, with sometimes dramatic results.

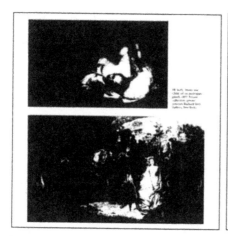

Image compositing permits better color reproduction while still enabling black and white text to be rendered "crisply," as demonstrated in the example above.

It is worth pausing for a moment to reflect on the evolution of the practice of digital archiving as we begin to take steps toward preserving the huge body of content that is now 'born digital,' that is, produced with online display and use in mind (even if there is still a print version). The fundamental principles still apply: online works need to be kept secure, accessible, and capable of conversion to successor technologies. But the standard of faithful replication will not apply at all well in the archiving of born-digital content, which is inherently less stable. Many questions about the practical aspects of archiving and rendering born-digital content remain to be settled by the community. The very definitions or boundaries of an 'article,' an 'issue,' and a 'journal' in an online context are still subject to considerable debate and rapid change. This presents special challenges for electronic archives such as ensuring the integrity of online documents, signaling readers clearly about the provenance and authenticity of content they encounter, ascertaining what constitutes 'completeness' in an article or journal run, and maintaining the crucial intellectual value of the works being archived for posterity.

Our sister organization, Portico, has already begun to confront the many questions surrounding archiving of born-digital works. The Portico archiving service launched in 2005 with Elsevier and several other publishers agreeing to participate. JSTOR and Portico are collaborating to think through and develop solutions to a host of digital archiving issues ranging from archiving and rendering practices to sustainability issues. JSTOR has developed the initial display capability for the Portico launch, and will apply these early lessons to our own work on rendering the born-digital works of JSTOR participating publishers.

Usage

There have been pleasant surprises along the path that JSTOR has trod. For one thing, usage has far outpaced all predictions and expectations. In 2000, we thought a few million accesses was a lot, but by 2005, JSTOR received 250 million significant accesses! Digitizing older content turns out to have given it a second life. The second related surprise is how many smaller libraries have chosen to participate in JSTOR. This is primarily because the archive fills out collections and enables newer libraries to build a rich legacy collection faster and at lower cost than they ever could have in print.

Usage statistics for JSTOR can be difficult to interpret. Figure 5 shows total significant accesses of the archive over several years and the increases are indeed dramatic. The chart details 4 broad categories of access: browse, search, page views, and article downloads. While all categories have increased substantially over the period, searches and page views experienced the most dramatic upturns in 2005. Overall, usage has increased by an average of about 50% each year since 2001, but it is perhaps most interesting that 2005 exhibits even stronger usage growth than the previous year, suggesting that the increases have not yet peaked.

FIGURE 5. Total Significant Accesses 1997-2005

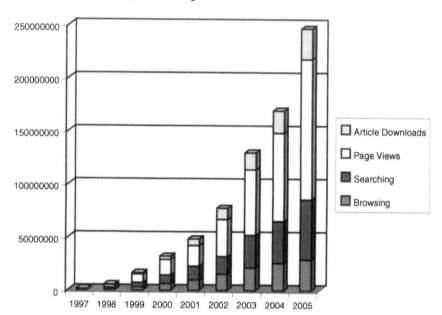

The next few charts look a bit deeper into these statistics to learn more about the breadth and depth of usage of content in JSTOR. Figure 6 shows usage by JSTOR classification, and demonstrates, not surprisingly, that the larger institutions tend to be the heavier users of JSTOR. We will revisit the question of value as it applies across the spectrum of institutions in the next section, but the sharp differences in usage shown here are a clear indication of the need in a community-based project like JSTOR to match the financial support we require from institutions to the value of the resource to them, even though we do not (and have no plans to) price directly according to usage.

Another take on usage is to look at the usage by discipline, as illustrated in Figure 7. Disciplinary usage is, of course, driven in part by how many practitioners and students there are in a given field. A second factor is how many titles, with what length 'pedigrees' we have in the archive. One would not expect highly specialized fields to attract high volumes of use. This, of course, has no bearing on the value of that use–so at JSTOR we are very cautious about drawing conclusions

FIGURE 6. Usage by Classification

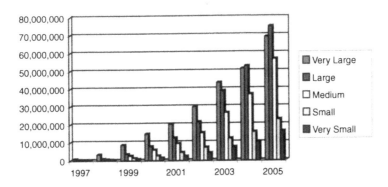

FIGURE 7. Usage of Titles by Discipline

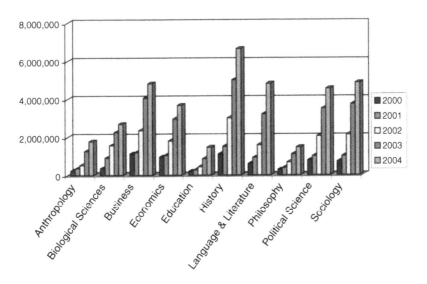

solely from the sheer volume of use. For example, an article on basic economics used in an entry level course is likely to receive much more usage than will a specialized mathematics article–yet both might be considered of high value to the users. Nevertheless, usage is quite high across a spectrum of disciplines from Biological Sciences to Economics, and from Business to History and Language & Literature.

Interpreting the increases in use of the JSTOR archive is a risky task, because there are so many varied and complicating factors that contribute to increased usage. Among these variables are the continuous increases in the number of participating institutions, and the ongoing addition of content both in titles already archived (as the moving wall goes forward) and in new titles. Another factor is the addition of linking partners, some of which have dramatic impact. To try to get past the influence of these variables, we conducted a study in 2004 to learn whether there is, in addition to all these factors, any growth in the 'base' usage of the content. That is, if we eliminate the usage associated with new content and new participating institutions, has there been increased usage? In Figure 8, we isolate the printing and downloading usage of the first Arts and Sciences collection at charter institutions that had participated in that collection since at least 1999, when it was completed. We found that same-library, same-collection usage increased by approximately 26% between calendar year 2001 and calendar year 2003, notwithstanding the overall usage increases mentioned above. These figures do not account for the addition of 'moving wall' content because we cannot easily isolate the usage of that subset of the content from the usage of other content in the collection; however, we do know that new content added to the collection represents a much smaller portion of the total content in that collection than the 26% growth in usage.

The fact that the archive is accessed so often is, of course, one indicator of usefulness. But as readers' expectations for online capabilities change, JSTOR must offer tools and features that facilitate their work.

FIGURE 8. Same Institution, Same Content Usage 2001-2003

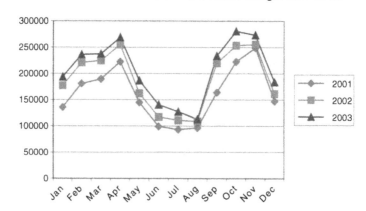

The reference linking project begun in 2005 is the most comprehensive upgrade to the archive to date. In the early days of JSTOR, it was prohibitively expensive to capture accurately the citations found in footnotes and endnotes of many articles. This meant that we were unable to create direct hyperlinks from the page image out to a referenced work, or even programmatically to recognize the presence of a citation in many cases, regardless of whether the cited work appeared in JSTOR or not. Since that time, the myriad benefits of reference linking have become apparent, and now this capability is a de facto standard for many scholarly resources online. Even today, however, most hyperlinking occurs from structured text rather than from image-based pages. This means that reference linking presents a special challenge for resources like JSTOR. In 2005, we began a project to rescan each page containing reference links, parsing the citation into its essential data elements, and capturing coordinates to indicate the position of the reference on the page. This project will take about two years altogether to complete for the entire 20 million page archive, but we are posting the links as they become available. The project has been on a preview site since December, and this first set of links was released to the public site on February 28, 2006.

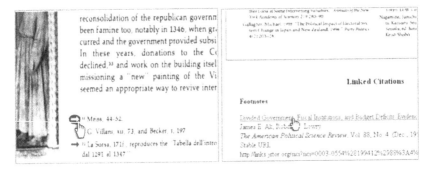

A citation link is indicated on the page image by an arrow. Linked citations are also included as structured text links at the bottom of each article.

Affordability and Value

Usage alone does not prove value. As noted earlier, we do not assume that a journal or discipline receiving relatively low usage is an indicator of poor value. After all, how would one calculate the value of a researcher locating a crucial insight in an obscure article that may lead to new findings or greater intellectual contributions? Like the famous credit card commercials, we might be inclined to answer: "Priceless!"

But when libraries are forced to allocate tight resources, they have little choice but to conduct cost/benefit analyses. Figures 9 and 10 provide a high level assessment of the cost borne by the library community to support JSTOR's archiving efforts and ensure ongoing access through JSTOR for their constituents. One pleasing aspect of these figures, of course, is that as the archive and community participation have grown, the average cost per institution for maintaining the content and accessing it has steadily declined.

Averages can be deceiving, so we look at value in much more detail. The next series of figures (Figures 11, 12, and 13) shows the cost per use figures for 10 institutions at the highest, median, and lowest levels of usage over a three-year period, and further breaks down those figures by institutional classification. We can see that the trend of decreasing cost per use holds true for all categories at the high and median levels of use. At the very lowest levels of use we become concerned about the economic value of participation. In this slide, it is apparent that the larger institutions experienced very modest and declining cost per use even at low usage levels, but the medium to very small institutions incurred increasing costs over the period studied.

We are not satisfied with these outcomes, though this is only one metric for assessing value. Even for these institutions, the cost per use might compare reasonably closely to the cost of online pay-per-view or

FIGURE 9. Cost Per Archived Title Per Institution

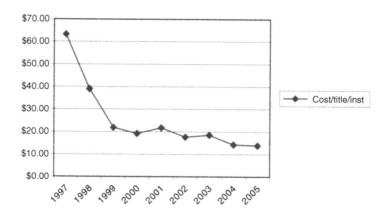

FIGURE 10. Average Cost Per Article Use

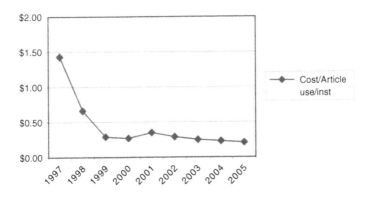

FIGURE 11. Average Cost/Use Top Ten Users by Classification

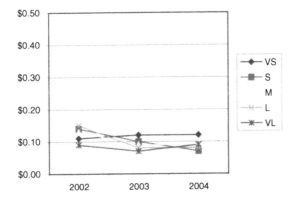

of ILL, for some types of articles, and they may be pleased with the value derived from relying upon JSTOR for preservation, collection completeness, and convenience.

We will continue to monitor these sorts of benchmarks, and will look for opportunities to work with librarians to improve the value they receive from participation in JSTOR. At the very least we note that, in general, these figures are very strong indicators that the original motivating idea behind JSTOR was correct: community-based action can be more economical, and create greater value system-wide.

FIGURE 12. Average Cost/Use Median Ten Users by Classification

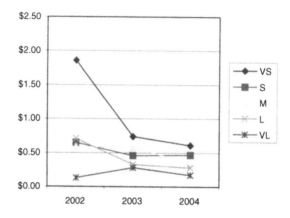

FIGURE 13. Average Cost/Use Lowest Ten Users by Classification

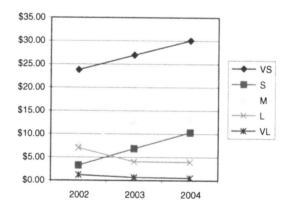

Still, the figures here do not show that libraries are actually saving money on shelf space or on the labor of cataloguing and reshelving print materials. There was certainly a period when librarians understandably felt constrained from even considering removing legacy journals to remote storage. Too many of their constituents were still attached to the look and feel of print, and there was still uncertainty about the durability of online archives. But there are now clear signs that some libraries are beginning to realize the potential savings enabled by JSTOR and other online resources.

In 2004, Dan Greenstein of the University of California estimated that the system of 10 universities could save some $5 million by combining storage and reducing duplicate print copies of journals found in the JSTOR archive. He wrote:

> Cost avoidance . . . is available for legacy print holdings that are accessible online. JSTOR comprises online back-runs for some 400 scholarly journals. The UC libraries possess, on average, seven copies for each of the 23,000 volumes in the JSTOR collection. A single print archive could be assembled from the UC libraries' current holdings for around $550,000. By eliminating their duplicate copies, the libraries could then save up to $5.3 million a year in the capital cost of shelving.
>
> Daniel Greenstein, *EDUCAUSE Review*, vol. 39, no. 5 (September/October 2004): 72-73

Today, the University of California system is one of the print repository partners for JSTOR and is beginning to realize some of those promised savings. This move was considered very carefully by the librarians in the system, and their deliberation appears to have paid off.

California is certainly not the only example. Last year, The Chronicle of Higher Education reported on The University of Texas at Austin removing some 90,000 volumes from its shelves that it is able to supply electronically. The only critical comment the Chronicle was able to garner was from a student who expressed a preference for the look and feel of print. This type of concern has been heard from the earliest days of online publishing, and undoubtedly explains the persistence of print, at least in part.

Will these cost-saving actions by libraries to embrace the digital age become more widespread? Will they provide lasting savings or only prove to deliver a one-time benefit to the libraries who engage in them? These very important and interesting questions remain to be answered in time.

CONCLUSIONS:
TOWARD AN ONLINE SCHOLARLY
COMMUNICATIONS SYSTEM

Even if libraries ultimately find that their legacy print collections can be discarded or stored remotely in order to save money, a potentially larger question looms, and is perhaps the core question of this conference: Do libraries need print subscriptions at all anymore or can much greater savings be realized by accepting content delivered only online? Many wise observers have noted that the much-vaunted lowering of journal subscription prices promised by online publishing has not in fact occurred. Publishers rightly point out that they have not realized any savings–journals still must be printed in non-economical print runs to meet subscription obligations; meanwhile, online publishing has its own demands and expenses.

From a broad community perspective, it is increasingly apparent that online delivery of scholarly works offers more advantages than print publishing alone. Even setting aside the potential cost savings, there are many reasons for the community to continue with the historic transition that is already under way. The incremental cost of providing more access is far lower than that for print. Digital content lends itself to saving, transfer, searching, and processing better than paper as well, and these capabilities, we are beginning to understand, can lead to new forms of research, collaboration, and communication.

We have moved from famine to feast with respect to digitization of legacy content as well as the production of new born-digital content. Many publishers have begun to create new online products from their back files. These take many forms from complete back runs of single titles to article collections in one discipline across a number of titles from one publisher. The business models are equally diverse, as publisher offers range from free access online, to including back issues with a current issue subscription, to one-time fees for the archive only, to separate annual subscriptions for current and legacy content. Besides the publishers' activities, there are many ongoing digitization efforts among libraries, and, of course, there are also mass digitization projects funded by Google, MSN, or Yahoo!. In short, there is much activity, all of it worthy and potentially useful.

What further obstacles remain in the path toward fully realizing the benefits and savings of broad online content availability?

The prospect of abandoning print continues to have worrisome aspects that are not resolved. Don Waters, a friend of JSTOR and a program officer at the Andrew W. Mellon Foundation, has noted, with some alarm, the significance of libraries moving from ownership of a print artifact to licensing of a more ephemeral electronic resource: "The shift to electronic publication in its current form represents a dramatic, jump-off-the-cliff shift in the academy from owning scholarly output to effectively renting it" (Don Waters, *Managing Digital Assets in Higher Education: An Overview of Strategic Issues*, p. 9 (WORK IN PROGRESS–presented at October, 2005 ARL meeting)). Don is not suggesting that print should be retained merely in order to ensure that the academy maintains an ownership stake in the outputs of scholarly endeavor. Rather, he is noting the urgency for the community to attend to archiving and intellectual property rights by developing solutions from within the academy.

While we're on the topic of ownership, there is another trend that seems to point in a different direction, toward a sort of return of ownership of intellectual property rights to the authors and researchers who originate the work, rather than signing over the rights to publishers. This issue is somewhat orthogonal to the question of whether and how we transition away from print, but it seems to arise with particular force in an online environment. Online publishing has low barriers to entry, and invites new forms of collaboration. These structural features, while beneficial, will almost certainly lead to confusion about ownership and rights issues. There is a good case for authors to retain certain rights in their work. Some publishers may have unduly restricted the uses of works, even by the original author, after obtaining copyright. But publisher behavior isn't the main issue. Authors will need to retain copyright, or at very least broad licenses, in order to supply works to institutional repositories and other appropriate entities. Confusion will arise as the definition of an 'article' evolves and more contributors may hold rights to some aspect of an online work. This so-called 'balkanization' of rights can lead to intractable permissioning complexities, not only for publishers wanting to repurpose works or license them to aggregators and other entities, but for third party archives such as JSTOR with a mission to be stewards of scholarly content.

A related issue has to do with 'fair use' and the new research opportunities presented by electronic content. Joe Esposito, in a seminal 2003 article called "The Processed Book" ("The processed book," Joseph J. Esposito, *First Monday*, volume 8, number 3 (March 2003), URL: http://firstmonday.org/issues/issue8_3/esposito/index.html), wrote about the unique value of online works and the way they are changing and will change scholarship. Not only are works becoming more collaborative, but there are new opportunities for research that arise from the nature of electronic content. Since it can be 'processed,' we may find new insights through text and data mining that were simply not within our capabilities to perform with print works. And works can be more easily transformed and manipulated, edited and annotated, leading to still more possibilities . . . and still more challenges.

On another note, Cliff Lynch has commented that the availability of inexpensive storage and good search capabilities may render 'curatorial' activities obsolete. I think Cliff is right that there may be no need literally to weed, or discard, digital objects; but curation in the sense of selection still plays a role, I would contend, in helping human researchers sift through an enormous body of work to locate the most important or most relevant. Of course, it is possible that 'curation' will increasingly be aided by 'processing' tools, and may become increasingly a personal rather than an institutional activity. I would like to ponder whether that really is so, or whether organizations like publishers, librarians, and, for that matter, JSTOR, will have a continuing role in helping achieve community consensus about what is accurate, relevant, and innovative in the vast and growing sea of content that exists and will be saved online.

How does JSTOR facilitate the transition from print to electronic publishing? JSTOR is working to provide some of the community infrastructure that will be necessary for libraries and publishers to be confident in moving forward with the transition. Specifically, we have demonstrated the value to scholars of placing our community's intellectual legacy online, and have shown that we will keep developing new capabilities to facilitate the work of researchers. Furthermore, JSTOR continues to monitor evolving standards and initiate practical solutions for archiving in the digital age. Last year, in helping to launch Portico, we extended the infrastructure available and opportunities to support preservation to include not only titles selected for JSTOR, but a much broader set of materials being relied upon by students and scholars.

The scholarly community has a fine and strong tradition of sharing information and collaborating for the public good that should put us in a good position to clear the remaining hurdles and to embrace the unique opportunities presented by the digital age. We at JSTOR look forward to continuing our close involvement with the international academic community to find balanced solutions to the intellectual property and technological challenges we all face.

doi:10.1300/J111v46n02_05

The Library and the Newsstand:
Thoughts on the Economics
of News Preservation

Bernard F. Reilly, Jr.

SUMMARY. Libraries have traditionally fulfilled an important and unique role in aggregating and preserving newspapers from all regions of the world. European and American research libraries have thus guaranteed survival of a rich cultural and historical record of all world regions. Online "newspapers" and electronic aggregation of news content have changed the way news is distributed and used, and rendered the established model for preservation ineffective. The availability to future researchers of much of today's news content is thus imperiled. The problem can be surmounted by new paradigms for preservation. doi:10.1300/J111v46n02_06 *[Article copies available for a fee from The Haworth Document Delivery Service: 1-800-HAWORTH. E-mail address: <docdelivery@haworthpress.com> Website: <http://www.HaworthPress.com> © 2007 by The Haworth Press, Inc. All rights reserved.]*

KEYWORDS. News, newspapers, online news, preservation, mass media, developing world, history, political ideology, Google, Internet

Bernard F. Reilly, Jr., is President, Center for Research Libraries, 6050 South Kenwood Avenue, Chicago, IL 60637-2804 (E-mail: reilly@crl.edu).

Paper delivered at the conference Printed Resources and Digital Information: The Future of Coexistence, University of Oklahoma, March 2006.

[Haworth co-indexing entry note]: "The Library and the Newsstand: Thoughts on the Economics of News Preservation." Reilly, Jr., Bernard F. Co-published simultaneously in *Journal of Library Administration* (The Haworth Information Press, an imprint of The Haworth Press, Inc.) Vol. 46, No. 2, 2007, pp. 79-85; and: *Print vs. Digital: The Future of Coexistence* (ed: Sul H. Lee) The Haworth Information Press, an imprint of The Haworth Press, Inc., 2007, pp. 79-85. Single or multiple copies of this article are available for a fee from The Haworth Document Delivery Service [1-800-HAWORTH, 9:00 a.m. - 5:00 p.m. (EST). E-mail address: docdelivery@haworthpress.com].

It is a commonplace that a healthy news industry is essential to an informed citizenry. Less well known is the critical supporting role that libraries have played for the past two centuries in exposing members of Western society to a broad range of news and opinion. Libraries have traditionally been repositories of a wide variety of viewpoints, particularly minority viewpoints, and of a multiplicity of information sources as contained in the output of the world's presses. With the deployment of digital technologies for disseminating news, economic and legal factors have now come into play that are eroding the longstanding symbiotic relationship between libraries and the news media. Unless countered, those factors threaten to impoverish public discourse today and our collective memory tomorrow.

The news industry is one of the great institutions of modern society. A product of the rise of the urban middle class, newspapers from the outset have achieved a happy union of information and commerce. They are an encyclopedic record of the daily events, accomplishments, ideas, and aspirations of their communities, whose assembly and distribution are largely subsidized by advertisers eager to reach a wide audience. If the record is skewed or biased at times, it is nonetheless the product of an elaborate system of checks and balances that the journalistic profession has evolved over time. News provides, in Ben Bradlee's words, a "first rough draft of history."

While newspapers deliver an enormous amount of information to millions daily their circulation is, with a few notable exceptions, relatively localized and their shelf-life brief. Libraries know no such limitations: they gather newspapers from near and far, their holdings dwarfing those of the local newsstand. In the early nineteenth century, as news vendors in the streets peddled the *Herald, Tribune, Globe, Sun*, and other mass-market titles, broadsheets of the radical abolitionist movement were gathered and perused in the reading rooms of the small subscription libraries and lycea of New York, Boston, and Philadelphia. These institutions existed to satisfy the demands of Americans of modest means for ideas and views outside the mainstream. It was in newspapers like *The Charter Oak* and *The Liberator* that the germ of the idea of the unconditional abolition of slavery in the United States was first nurtured, an idea that decades later helped sweep the nation into Civil War.

In the twentieth century the academic libraries and research libraries have fulfilled a similar function, gathering news from around the world to promote "current awareness" and satisfy students and learners hungry for intelligence from their home regions or subjects of study. Newspapers have always heralded the earliest stirrings of new political movements and ideologies. They fueled the anti-apartheid movement in southern Africa, and carried abroad the idea of independence for India to Diaspora communities as far afield as Seattle and Geneva, Switzerland, forty years before England was forced to grant statehood to the subcontinent.[1] (Newspapers are the harbingers, if not vehicles, of toxic ideologies as well: in Cambodia where the Khmer-language newspapers of the 1950s and '60s tracked the rise of Khmer Rouge ideology in the decades leading up to the killing fields of the 1970s.)

While even the largest of these libraries, NYPL, Harvard, Library of Congress, British Library, represent a trivial, secondary market for news and a relatively small source of revenue for the publishers, they have traditionally aggregated a far more diverse array of content–and opinion, than their counterparts the newsstands. And while the shelves of the newsstand are cleared nightly to make way for the influx of the next morning's editions, newspapers remain on the shelves of the library and, when eventually retired, are carefully filed away to await rediscovery by subsequent generations of consumers.

Preserving yesterday's news for future generations, libraries enlarge the readership base of newspapers over time, while relieving the publishers of the burden (and cost) of maintaining and servicing their back runs.

This symbiotic relationship between library and newsstand has enabled the great American and European research libraries to preserve newspapers from regions where infrastructure for the dissemination and preservation of news is underdeveloped, and from places where dictatorial regimes control or undermine such infrastructure. Libraries in Europe and the United States have functioned as proxy national libraries for various countries in Latin America, sub-Saharan Africa, the Middle East, and South Asia, preserving essential cultural and historical evidence by gathering and archiving the output of the regions' presses. With this useful division of labor between library and newsstand news production has flourished and libraries have been able to ensure the survival of a rich record of the world's events and a broad spectrum of ideas and opinion. Private interest and public good were in equilibrium.

Today the World Wide Web is becoming the newsstand of choice, or convenience. A June 2005 national survey conducted by the Pew Research Center for the People & the Press indicates that newspaper readership is dwindling. According to the Pew report "a third of Americans below age 40 cite the internet as their main source of news, and many of these people are reading newspapers online." The report also notes that people under age 50 are far less likely to read a print newspaper than are older people, but they are reading newspapers online in "fairly significant numbers."[2]

If the Web is the global newsstand of the future, what becomes of the age-old synergy between newsstand and library? As newspapers go the way of . . . the afternoon newspaper, will libraries continue to ensure that a wide spectrum of diverse sources and opinion survives? The answer is, probably not. As readers rely increasingly on the Web for news, libraries are no longer preserving news to the extent to which they once did. As paper subscriptions dwindle the formidable stacks of newsprint that once piled up on library shelves are disappearing, and libraries have not yet figured out how to archive the Web effectively and systematically.

Is this a problem? Many maintain that the library's function has been supplanted by the Web and by Internet search engines like Google, Yahoo! and by the massive knowledge aggregators like Lexis-Nexis, NewsBank, and Factiva. The search engines in fact do fulfill many traditionally library functions: they organize knowledge, and make it available and discoverable. Moreover the Web now surpasses any single library in the amount of current news and opinion it offers, and its content is continually growing. Every day the aggregators ingest, process, and index news from thousands of sources worldwide, and deliver it to a range of devices from desktops to cell phones to PDAs, in a variety of formats—services arguably superior to the best that libraries are equipped to offer.

However, the behaviors of the search engines and aggregators suggest that to view them as a substitute for libraries we are in danger of losing something important. Trust, for one, given the recent willingness of the search engine companies to cooperate with Chinese government censors to block access to political Web sites. With libraries censorship is never an issue. In the U.S. librarians have strenuously and, for the most part successfully, resisted government and public interference. Witness the American Library Association's recent active opposition to reauthorization of the USA Patriot Act. With the exception perhaps of the odd presidential library, libraries are disinterested repositories, dedicated to maintaining intact society's historical and cultural record for future scholars and other stakeholders yet unborn.

Even more likely to compromise the integrity and diversity of this record, however, are the economics of news production and distribution. The growing consolidation of the news media and the increasingly tight control over rights exercised by those media in the electronic environment are weakening a critical link in our society's chain of evidence.

News media consolidation is narrowing the spectrum of news and opinion that is reported today, creating homogeneity of content that will impoverish the historical record.

Most news maintained by the aggregators is recent news and news of interest to the largest possible constituency. The most lucrative markets for news are the global financial and legal industries, the national security apparatus, and the mass-market consumer. The aggregators trade in information on people and places of international significance or that interest large consumer populations. They are more likely to provide sensational details of the Michael Jackson trial or the breakup of Time Warner than chronicle the emergence of a new strain of jihadist belief in Southeast Asia or political struggle of tin miners in Bolivia.

As market economics prevail in the news industry, ideological diversity is being marginalized and pushed out to the Web. Minority viewpoints are alive and well on the Web. If the struggles against slavery, apartheid, or British dominion in India were waged today their battle for public opinion would take place on the Web.

In both cases important information will probably have only a brief shelf life. Despite the lengthening tail of content's value over time there may be insufficient incentive for commercial organizations, like their earlier counterparts the newsstands, to maintain much news content after its value in this market is exhausted. If we rely on the commercial news vendors and aggregators to maintain this content for scholars, there will be sizable gaps in the historical and cultural record.

And the efforts by libraries to archive the Web have been only sporadic and unsystematic. The artifacts of the Zapatistas' early struggle in Mexico–the Web sites and electronic message boards that they and their supporters used to gain international attention and support–are vanished. The ephemeral character of the Web increasingly undermines the ability of public policy scholars to invoke critical evidence for their assertions and arguments. An examination of recent reports produced by two of the most authoritative policy research organizations, the Brookings Institution's and Library of Congress Federal Research Division, reveals an astonishing degree of reliance upon Web-based documents and sources that are no longer "live." The chain of evidence has been broken.

Meanwhile, it seems that the safety net traditionally provided by libraries is fraying badly. A recent survey of major research libraries by the International Coalition on Newspapers, a project funded by the NEH and the Center for Research Libraries, found that with current news easily accessed on the Web, libraries are radically reducing their subscriptions to foreign newspapers. Moreover, under enormous pressure to devote less shelf space to paper and more funds to electronic resources, even the largest research libraries are divesting of newspaper backfiles.

What is at risk is not only the comprehensiveness of the historical record but its richness. Just as scale drives homogeneity in consumer products, the economics of the information market threatens to turn our libraries into Wal-Marts.

Clearly, there is no going back to the era of dim, musty reading rooms and card catalogs. Today, Google, Yahoo!–and Baidu–are the channels through which students and scholars discover and access source materials. Libraries are no longer just the places where people seek the world's information. People no longer need such places. Information won't be localized.

The critical role for libraries in today's society is to be not places but agents. Libraries must actively work to preserve the "biodiversity" of ideas, opinions, and cultures. In this role they have been set back on their heels by restrictive positions regarding copyright taken by the media and creative industries. By acting assertively they are capable of achieving a new symbiosis with the news industry.

News organizations must be willing to grant libraries rights to make the limited, specific digital uses of their intellectual property that can enable archiving and survival of this knowledge in electronic form from one generation to the next. This will require ceding to libraries the relatively small, scholarly markets that libraries have always served and which were always merely secondary to the publishers' interests. This would be a useful departure from the adversarial stance that media organizations have lately taken to libraries.

The costly work of preserving electronic news should be supported by the national government and the private sector as well. The major international NGOs and foundations like UNESCO, Carnegie, Ford, Rockefeller, and others should recognize as development activity the enormous historic investment that U.S. and European universities and libraries have made to preserve the world's memory. These institutions have been supporting development of technologies and skills for delivering medical, legal, and other practical information to local populations in emerging regions. But this neglects the investment needed to ensure the availability of historical and cultural evidence vital to the identity needed to promote civility in those societies. A strong case can be made for supporting libraries' efforts to electronically "repatriate" the critical evidence and materials that they have gathered and maintained for the last two centuries, and which are essential to cultural identity–and accountability–in societies from Chile to Zimbabwe.

Institutions that preserve news on a large scale, like the Center for Research Libraries and the American Antiquarian Society, struggle perennially as an increasing share of higher education funding goes to the sciences. Because funding will always be scarce, such organizations will have to enlist greater support from individual libraries. Supporting digital delivery of the "old paper" news content will enable American libraries not only to make the great legacy materials they have accumulated over the years available to source communities, but to spread the cost of doing so over a wider population. This support must be in the form of funding and, equally important, relinquishing some local control and ownership of collection materials to avoid redundancy. This investment will be necessary just to stay in place and achieve what libraries accomplished individually in the past.

This agenda can all be accomplished with existing technologies. The question is not whether libraries will abandon their vital function in society of providing an enduring record of diverse points of view, but whether we will abandon libraries by failing to recognize and support them in this role.

NOTES

1. Irene Joshi, "South Asian Newspapers." Paper presented as part of the Symposium on Access to and Preservation of Global Newspapers, May 27-28, 1997, Washington DC <http://www.lib.washington.edu/southasia/iconpaper.html>.

2. <http://people-press.org/reports/display.php3?ReportID=248> The report continues, "One-in-four (24%) list the internet as a main source of news. Roughly the same number (23%) say they go online for news every day, up from 15% in 2000; the percentage checking the web for news at least once a week has grown from 33% to 44% over the same time period."

doi:10.1300/J111v46n02_06

The Digital Difference
in Reference Collections

Michael K. Buckland

SUMMARY. One of the very first digital library developments was the transition of bibliographies to digital formats and the rise of online services which allowed new kinds of searching for topics. Here we examine three other reference genres: (1) Gazetteers, which, when coupled with maps and bibliographies, allow new ways to search by place; (2) Chronologies, which when digitized and combined with time lines and named time periods, transform search by time; and (3) Biographical directories, which, with improved design, could link persons with their contexts in new and more effective ways. The paper will present work developed in a project entitled: Support for the Learner: What, Where, When, and Who. doi:10.1300/J111v46n02_07 *[Article copies available for a fee from The Haworth Document Delivery Service: 1-800-HAWORTH. E-mail address: <docdelivery@haworthpress.com> Website: <http://www.HaworthPress.com> © 2007 by The Haworth Press, Inc. All rights reserved.]*

Michael K. Buckland is Professor, Information Management and Systems, and Co-Director, Electronic Cultural Atlas Initiative, University at California, Berkeley, 102 South Hall #4600, Berkeley, CA 94720-4600 (E-mail: buckland@berkeley.edu).

Paper for Conference on Printed Resources and Digital Information: The Future of Coexistence, Oklahoma University Libraries. March 2 & 3, 2006.

This paper draws on the work of many people, especially Aitao Chen, Fredric C. Gey, Ray R. Larson, and Vivien Petras, in three projects partially supported by the Institute of Museum and Library services through two National Leadership grants: Seamless Searching of Numeric and Textual Resources (award 178, 1999-2002), Going Places in the Catalog: Improved Geographic Access (LG-02-02-0035-02, 2002-04), and Support for the Learner (LG-02-04-0041-04, 2004-06).

[Haworth co-indexing entry note]: "The Digital Difference in Reference Collections." Buckland, Michael K. Co-published simultaneously in *Journal of Library Administration* (The Haworth Information Press, an imprint of The Haworth Press, Inc.) Vol. 46, No. 2, 2007, pp. 87-100; and: *Print vs. Digital: The Future of Coexistence* (ed: Sul H. Lee) The Haworth Information Press, an imprint of The Haworth Press, Inc., 2007, pp. 87-100. Single or multiple copies of this article are available for a fee from The Haworth Document Delivery Service [1-800-HAWORTH, 9:00 a.m. - 5:00 p.m. (EST). E-mail address: docdelivery@haworthpress.com].

KEYWORDS. Reference collections, subject bibliographies, gazetteers, search terms, reference service, searching online, topic vocabularies, cross references, chronologies and online searching, biographical directories

INTRODUCTION

My topic is the reference collection. Somehow the reference collection does not seem to have made an effective transition to the digital networked environment. This is surprising because online searching of bibliographies and reference works was one of the first and most powerful drivers of libraries' transition to a digital networked environment and now there is a lot of work on the development of software to help reference librarians to provide reference help remotely. But the best kind of help is self-help and here we are concerned with the reference *collection.*

I have spent many happy and productive hours using reference collections. The needs served by a reference collection have not gone away. What happened to the reference collection in the transition to a digital library environment? And what, if anything, should be done next?

New technology does not change the mission of a library. It simply opens up alternative means: new procedures for the same purpose. So what is the purpose of a reference collection? The reference collection is composed of a set of resources selected to serve two needs:

1. Looking up or verifying factual data, often referred to as "ready reference"; and
2. Establishing an initial outline and *context* for any topic efficiently and effectively, especially determining the what, where, when, and who aspects of whatever is of interest.

Libraries are concerned with education. The difference between memorizing and understanding is that understanding means knowing the context. This is what sir Francis Bacon meant when he said "Knowledge is power." Knowledge is power because, if you understand context and relationships, then you know how to make things happen, and knowing how to make things happen is a form of power.

When a student, a journalist, or a researcher is curious about some topic or event, a traditional strategy is to seek the "5Ws and the H" of investigative writing: What, Where, When, Who, Why, and How. In the past, when libraries were on paper, after one had exhausted the few out-of-date reference books at home, the next step would be to go to the local college or public library. And there one would find a wonderful amenity: a carefully selected collection of the library's best and most up-to-date reference works carefully pre-arranged. There would be a biography section, with biographical dictionaries and Who's Whos, to help with WHO questions. Also, a history section with almanacs and chronologies designed to help with WHEN questions, and a geography section with atlases and place name gazetteers to help with WHERE. For WHAT there would be general and specialized dictionaries and encyclopedias, and the subject headings in the nearby catalog designed to lead to more. WHY and HOW are less straightforward, but the basic structure was well-designed for WHAT, WHERE, WHEN, and WHO, as shown in Figure 1. In a paper-based environment the reference collection plays an important role, but that helpful structure is largely absent, or, at least, less prominent, in the digital library environment.

REFERENCE COLLECTIONS
IN A DIGITAL LIBRARY ENVIRONMENT

In a digital environment, one cannot see the collection. One cannot see beyond the screen, although an interface may provide some guidance. We no longer have the familiar pleasure of seeing a well-stocked collection, of being able to grasp the layout and to assess the relative size of each section, and recognize, at a glance, familiar tools that can provide answers. The valuable structured guidance of the arrangement of the reference collection and of each reference work is mostly absent.

FIGURE 1. Reference Genres and Their Features

Reference Genre	Vocabulary	Special displays	About
Dictionary, Encyclopedia	Topics	Cross-references	What
Atlas, Gazetteer	Places	Maps	Where
Almanac, Chronology	Time	Timelines	When
Biographical dictionary	Persons	Interpersonal relationships	Who

The indexes are not usually displayed and, even if browsing is supported, we usually cannot see much of the internal arrangement. Typically the cursor just winks in an empty search box.

This large gap in digital library service is ironic because one of the very first and most visible digital library developments was the transition of reference works, especially bibliographies, to digital formats, and the rise of online search services which allowed one to search reference works remotely. There is a lively literature now on "online reference," but it is concerned more with supporting the work of reference *librarians* rather than empowering self-service use of resources by library users.

The Internet Public Library has an attractive reference collection. If we look at it, we can see that it is a replica of the technology of the codex. There is a dominant hierarchical structure: Go to the collection; find the section; select a reference work; look in the index; find the detail desired. It is convenient in the sense that you can use it from anywhere, twenty-four hours a day, but it is weaker than the paper version in that you sometimes cannot browse the index. You may reach an empty query box and have to guess what term to use and how it is spelled. Then you climb back out and drill down again, one resource at a time, repeatedly, until you are satisfied or give up.

But digital reference does not have to be that way. If you are not using books you do not have to follow the constraints of the technology of the paper codex. Digital technology allows links to be direct and horizontal if two conditions are met: There needs to be *procedural interoperability*, of which the Z39:50 search and retrieve protocol is an example; and there needs to be *vocabulary interoperability*, of which Dewey's relative index to his decimal classification is an example.

TECHNOLOGY CHANGE

New technology brings more than technological change and ordinarily comes in two stages. At first the new technology is used to perform existing work in a new way: *to do the same things differently and better*. The earliest printers initially designed type that resembled manuscript writing. The more interesting change comes later in the second stage. With greater familiarity with the characteristics of the new technology, it becomes a matter of *doing better different things* (Buckland 1992). The reference collection presented in the Internet Public Library can be regarded as being in the first stage, a digital replica of the book-based environment: Doing the same thing differently and better. We can now consider the challenge of moving the reference collection into the second stage, going with the flow of digital technology to do different better things. To explore how that might be done we consider the second, more complex purpose of the reference collection, supporting the user's need to establish context by learning about What, Where, When, and Who, and relationships between them.

A series of studies at Berkeley indicates, I believe, how we might reconstruct the attractive functionality of the traditional reference collection in a digital environment. These studies were a collaboration between researchers in the School of Information (formerly the School of Library and Information Studies) and the Electronic Cultural Atlas Initiative (ECAI), an informal collaboration among scholars worldwide to advance education and research in the humanities and social sciences through increased attention to place and time (Buckland & Lancaster 2004). To understand human activities you have to know about the cultural context: What else had been happening in that community at that time. Further, time and place provide a unifying framework across all disciplines and provides an organizing principle for bringing together scholarly resources of many different kinds. The mission of ECAI is not to construct a single cultural atlas, but–a quite different agenda–to operate at multiple levels to advance academic best practices: Advocacy for attention to place and time; encouraging the development of infrastructure through collaboration, standards, and technology; and gaining practical experience and providing proof-of-concept. To the extent to which these goals are achieved and resources become network-accessible and interoperable, scholars will become able to compose temporally dynamic cultural maps for themselves drawing on each others' resources.

In what follows, we go back to basics and start with the assumption that the purpose of a reference collection is to provide answers to the four basic questions: What, Where, When, and Who. These four facets are different in kind. Distinct reference genres exist for each. Each has special display requirements (as shown in Figure 1) and, in practice, they are very closely entangled with each other.

WHAT–TOPIC LISTS– CROSS-REFERENCES WITHIN AND BETWEEN VOCABULARIES

Search and selection depends on categorization, which we use as a general term to include indexing, classification, and every other form of ordered arrangement. The forms vary–indexes, lists of subject headings, thesauri, category codes, classifications, and so on–but they are all descriptive vocabularies and traditionally were called, collectively, "documentary languages." As with natural languages, the meanings of terms evolve and vary between groups. The optimal choice of search term in any given resource may be unclear and a search term that works within one resource may not be the best term to use in another resource even for the same topic. We cope with these anomalies in a paper-based environment because we tend to use one resource at a time, because the number of resources available is usually small and stable, because a printed display of an index enables us to survey the options and overall arrangement, and because it is easier to recognize a topical name than to guess at it. For example, if we were interested in martial arts movies, one could recognize as relevant the Library of Congress Subject Heading "Hand-to-hand fighting, oriental, in motion pictures," but how many people would have imagined that as a heading to look under? We learn to navigate topic terminology with more or less success. A central feature of indexing and classification is the effort invested in internal consistency and much of the training is in how to establish cross-references within a thesaurus so as to achieve internal coherence.

There always have been two kinds of mapping: Documents are assigned (mapped) to categories, and our queries also have to be mapped to the categories. Library science has heavily emphasized the first and underestimated the importance of the second, even though Melvil Dewey thought that his relative index was at least as important as the decimal classification. Dewey considered his index to the classification to be at least as important as the classification itself because it would lead users from whatever words they were familiar with to the correct point in the unfamiliar "vocabulary" of classification numbers. One does not search effectively or economically in unfamiliar resources because learning to use resources effectively takes time and experience and is an important ingredient in effectiveness for scholar and reference librarian alike.

It is not good enough to assume that the use of verbal keywords resolves problems because language is dynamic, unstable, ambiguous, and multiple. Language, especially vocabulary, evolves in communities. That is why and how one can often tell where someone is from and what their occupation is from the words they use and the way they use them. It is a matter of dialect. In a paper environment variations of this type are not very difficult to handle. One can see the options displayed. One learns the foibles of different indexes. In a digital, network environment, the situation is different. First, the visual overview that we depend on in a print environment to familiarize ourselves with the vocabulary used is largely absent, even though some browsing may be supported. Second, the whole point of a network environment is to provide access to an ever-increasing range of distant resources. In a digital environment, both the collections and the indexing, although accessible, are more or less invisible behind the glowing screen, which leads to a paradox: the increase in network-accessible resources ensures that a growing number can be used, but also that a growing proportion of these resources are unfamiliar and so, if searched, will not be searched economically or effectively. For example, someone searching major resources for the topic *automobiles* will need to know to search under:

TL205 in the Library of Congress Classification,

180/280 in the U.S. Patent Classification,

3711 in the Standard Industrial Classification, and

PASS MOT VEH, SPARK IGN ENG in the U.S. federal import/export statistics.

This situation has a very important practical consequence. In teaching and in practice the emphasis is placed heavily on how to make cross-references *within* a thesaurus, but in a network environment where many resources are available, the situation changes. With a larger population of resources, the logic of the situation is to want to harvest from that larger and less familiar pool with less familiar categorization schemes and a third form of mapping, cross-references *between* thesauri, becomes more important relative to the cross-references *within* thesauri. You want to know not only the U.S. Patent Classification number for, say, *making peanut butter*, but also the (very different) corresponding International Patent Classification number, since moving from one to the other should be easier and smoother than in a paper environment.

A digital environment differs from a paper environment in its ability to support links *directly* between entries in different resources. It is no longer necessary to climb out of one work and then drill down into another to relate two entries. The whole point of a digital, network environment is to support search horizontally across many different resources. For this, cross-references *between* the different vocabularies of different databases become very important.

The outstanding example of mapping between different vocabularies is the Unified Medical Language System developed by the National Library of Medicine, a detailed topic mapping between numerous vocabularies in health and medicine. The problem, however, with the expert crafting of mappings between topic vocabularies is that it requires considerable expertise, is slow, expensive, and obsolescent, and does not scale. Fortunately, software techniques have been developed using statistical association and natural language processing which provide imperfect but useful mappings within minutes and at negligible cost if suitable training data are available (see Plaunt & Norgard 1998; Buckland et al. 1999).

SEARCHING ACROSS DIFFERENT MEDIA FORMS

In a digital environment, media forms other than text, such as images and statistical data series, are digitized. Here keywords and text searching are no longer feasible, as we found when we tried to bridge the gap between text resources and socio-economic numeric data series. It would be a welcome amenity if one could find both writings and statistical facts on the same topic. Any time you read an article it would be nice to be able go check how well the statistical evidence matched the written assertions. And if you found a startling statistical shift, it would be good library service to enable anyone to find out easily and quickly whether anyone had written about and explained the anomaly. But the simple keyword techniques of the text universe don't extend to other media forms. Suppose you find an intriguing number in a cell in a statistical table. You could copy that number into a Google search box and get a result, but it is very unlikely that the retrieved set would have anything to do with the statistical datum. The best that can be done is to use whatever textual description may be available in row labels, headers, captions, and elsewhere. Keyword searching of those words might work, but assigning topical headings from a well designed thesaurus will work much better–especially if the text resources also to be searched also use the same thesaurus or one that is or can be mapped to it.

Although different media cannot be linked directly, they can be linked indirectly through descriptive metadata. And, since different descriptive metadata are used in different environments, mapping between thesauri becomes all the more important as resources in multiple media become more common.

WHERE–PLACES–MAPS

For some purposes, *what* is not enough. For socio-economic statistical data series, for example, it is also ordinarily necessary to specify where. In bibliographies, as with catalogs, *place names* are typically used, which immediately creates two problems. First, "place" is a cultural construct and so inherently difficult to define; second, place *names* being part of natural language, have several problems. They:

- Have different forms, St. Petersburg, A,H,D$JD(, Sainte-Pétersbourg, etc.
- Are multiple: Cluj in Romania/Roumania/Rumania, is also Klausenburg and Kolosvar.
- Change: Bombay is now Mumbai.
- Are ambiguous: Numerous places named Beijing or Lafayette.
- Can be anachronistic. There was no country called Germany before 1870.
- May be vague, e.g., The MidWest, Far East, or Silicon Valley.

Further, there is a tendency to use political jurisdictions to define places, but political jurisdictions and their boundaries are themselves a bit unstable. Consider the Balkans and the former USSR.

Space, however, is a scientific construct and can be specified using the coordinates of latitude and longitude. Place and space constitute a dual naming system. Places can be defined in terms of the space they occupy and an important reference genre, the place name gazetteer, records these relationships, linking places with spaces.

A good gazetteer is a list of place names that also says what kind of place (geographic feature type) and gives spatial coordinates (latitude and longitude). These records show when similar names are for different places, when different names refer to the same place, and, most importantly, allow places to be shown on a map. In library parlance, gazetteers are place name authority files. If the place names in reference works were linked horizontally to their corresponding entries in online gazetteers, then there could be map-interfaces both for search results, showing visually the geographic dispersion of any set of records, but also as a device for expressing the geographic scope of a query, expressed as being within any hand-drawn area.

So, for example, a place name can be a dot on a map, the dot can be a link that can connect to a webpage about that place or generate a live query to search in other resources concerning this place. (For some examples, see ECAI Iraq (2003) and Going Places (2004).)

WHERE–TIME PERIOD–TIMELINE

Just as people tend to refer to locations in terms of *places* rather than *spaces*, so also, in both speech and writing, people tend to discuss time in terms of *events* rather than calendar dates. We use phrases such as, "after college," "during Vietnam," and "under Clinton." Time and events are mutually defining. Physical events are used to calibrate calendars and clocks. Calendars and clocks are, in turn, used to express the sequencing, duration, and intervals between events. There is, in effect, a dual naming system for *when* as well as for *where*, but, curiously, named time period directories, analogous to place name gazetteers, are hard to find. The analogy is close, however, so we designed and built a gazetteer-like time directory with the following components:

- Period name (e.g., Clinton administration, Weimar, Civil War);
- Period type (e.g., Reign, dynasty, war, natural disaster);
- Calendar time, specifying both calendar and dates; and
- Where this named period occurred. (This aspect is analogous to when a place name was in use.)

The symmetry in design and relationship with place name gazetteer is shown in Figure 2.

A prototype time period directory with some 2,000 entries was constructed by extracting chronological subdivisions from Library of Congress Subject Headings in library catalog records and adding the geographic field when not already present in the record. Three interfaces have been provided: Using lists of names of countries, of major cities, and, for some countries, states; a map with clickable countries, cities, and states; and a timeline interface (see Figure 3). When any named time period has been selected, users can click on a link to generate a live (Z39:50) search of the Library of Congress catalog to retrieved records for books concerning that period. (The searches work because the time period names are derived from properly formed subdivisions of subject headings.) Further, titles and, more especially, the subject headings of the catalog records retrieved indicate what topics and which individuals were important enough in that period to have books written about them (Petras, Larson & Buckland 2006) (see Figure 3).

FIGURE 2. Symmetry of Place Name Gazetteer and Time Period Directory

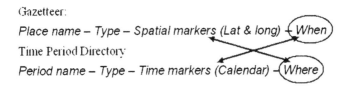

Gazetteer:

Place name – Type – Spatial markers (Lat & long) – When

Time Period Directory

Period name – Type – Time markers (Calendar) – Where

FIGURE 3. Time Line Interface to Time Period Directory, Sample Entry, and Live Query Link

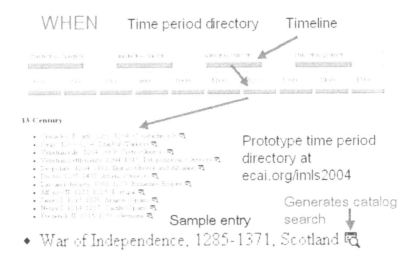

The Cheshire system interface was modified to display biographical subject headings separately in catalog records and embed an additional link from each name to search for a corresponding biographical article in the *Wikipedia* online encyclopedia (see Figure 4).

WHO–PERSONS–INTERPERSONAL RELATIONSHIPS

Biographical dictionaries and "Who's Whos" are a long established reference genre and they tend to follow similar styles, but moving biographical reference works into an online environment is hindered by

FIGURE 4. Query from Subject Heading of Retrieved Catalog Record to *Wikipedia* Article

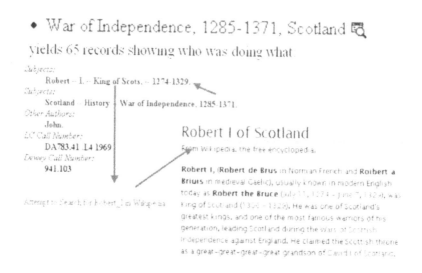

two major obstacles. First, formal standards for mark-up and even "best practices" appear to be a lacking, or, if used, remain proprietary and unpublicized. Even the experimental links from our time period directory to *Wikipedia* typically fail for lack of a common standard for form of personal name: Librarians invert (surname first in subject headings), and the *Wikipedia* does not in its filenames. A common standard or a standard conversion is required. Second, librarians, archivists, and bibliographers have focused on establishing authoritative files of personal names, not on the events in people's lives.

Nevertheless, the future use of biographical reference works in an online environment offers particularly exciting possibilities if only format, markup, and metadata could be made interoperable. The reason is that personal lives can be regarded as composed of a series of events (birth, marriage, death) and activities (study, occupation, creative work) each of which occurred during some point or span of time, in some place or places, and often involving other persons. Biographical texts are very densely packed with significant action statements, place names, dates and eras, the names of other persons and institutions, and references to documents. There are many internal links for these various aspects within the *Wikipedia*, but the real logic of digital technology would be to have links to other external resources. Subject headings exist for kinds of activities, gazetteers list places, time period directories can be used for eras, and biographical dictionaries list other people. Biographical text can be seen as epitomizing the potential digital difference in reference collections. When a place is named, it makes little sense to require the user to climb out of the biographical dictionary, locate the geography section, find a gazetteer, and then drill down into it to find the corresponding entry for that place, or to make a note of a mentioned document and take the details to a catalog to locate it. In a world of markup, metadata, and federated search protocols, the challenge is to re-design reference works in a digital environment to operate on a basis of lateral links in a formerly hierarchical environment.

We can consider this prospect as a reversal or inversion of the structure of the codex technology of the paper-based reference collection (see Figure 5).

CONCLUSION

Other speakers have discussed the need to replace or redesign undergraduate libraries and conventional reference desks to serve more effectively a generation of library users who prefer to search from their laptops, in their dorms, during the night, and, as far as they can, independently. The time is ripe for moving the *reference collection* to the

FIGURE 5. Reference Relationships in Paper and Digital Environments

Reference Genre	Vocabulary	Special displays	About
Dictionary, Encyclopedia	Topics	Cross-references	What
Atlas, Gazetteer	Places	Maps	Where
Almanac, Chronology	Time	Timelines	When
Biographical dictionary	Persons	Interpersonal relationships	Who

Reference genres and their features in a paper environment.

Reference Genre	Vocabulary	Special displays	About
What	Topics	Cross-references	Dictionary, Encyclopedia
Where	Places	Maps	Atlas, Gazetteer
When	Time	Timelines	Almanac, Chronology
Who	Persons	Interpersonal relationships	Biographical dictionary

Reference features and their genres in a digital environment.

second stage of technological change. Reference works are already largely digitized. The challenge is now to adapt the design of the reference works themselves to fit the already existing digital, networked environment of library users. Significant changes are overdue and suitable methods are already at hand to provide the digital difference in reference collections.

NOTE

Additional material can be found at and through the "Support for the Learner: What, Where, When, and Who" project website http://ecai.org/imls2004/.

REFERENCES

Buckland, M. *Redesigning Library Services: A Manifesto* (American Library Association, 1992). Available online at http://sunsite.berkeley.edu/Literature/Library/Redesigning/html.html. Visited Apr 9, 2006.

Buckland, M. & L. Lancaster. 2004. Combining time, place, and topic: The Electronic Cultural Atlas Initiative. *D-Lib Magazine* 10, no. 5 (May 2004). http://www.dlib.org/dlib/may04/buckland/05buckland.html. Visited Apr 9, 2006.

Buckland, M. et al. 1999. Mapping entry vocabulary to unfamiliar metadata vocabularies. *D-Lib Magazine* 5, no. 1 (Jan 1999). http://www. dlib.org/dlib/january99/buckland/01buckland.html. Visited Apr 9, 2006.

ECAI Iraq. 2003. http://ecai.org/iraq/. Visited Apr 9, 2006.

Going Places in the Catalog: Improved Geographic Access. 2004. http://ecai.org/imls2002/. Visited Apr 9, 2006.

Petras, Vivien, Ray R. Larson, Michael Buckland. "Time period directories: a metadata infrastructure for placing events in temporal and geographic context." *Proceedings of the 6th ACM/IEEE-CS joint conference on digital libraries 2006,* Chapel Hill, NC: 151-160.

Plaunt, C. & Norgard, B. A. 1998. An association based method for automatic indexing with a controlled vocabulary. *Journal of the American Society for Information Science.* 49, no.10 (August 1998):888-902. http://metadata.sims.berkeley.edu/assoc/assoc.html. Visited Apr 9, 2006.

doi:10.1300/J111v46n02_07

The Cooperative Conundrum
in the Digital Age

Dan Hazen

SUMMARY. Our prevailing models for library collections and collections cooperation emerged in the analog era. The electronic environment has changed the terms of both analysis and activity. This paper explores four aspects of the shift. The relationship between de facto systems and explicit cooperative frameworks, and the conceptual framework for library collections, reflect the mental models with which we structure our activities. Both require a new look. The Janus Conference, held at Cornell University in the fall of 2005, sought to recast the agenda for research library collections and cooperation in the digital age. The meeting's prospects and implications, as of the spring of 2006, are thus surveyed as well. Actual responses to these challenges, finally, are likely to play out differently across specific segments of our library community. This dynamic provides a final focus for comment. doi:10.1300/J111v46n02_08 *[Article copies available for a fee from The Haworth Document Delivery Service: 1-800-HAWORTH. E-mail address: <docdelivery@haworthpress.com> Website: <http://www.HaworthPress.com> © 2007 by The Haworth Press, Inc. All rights reserved.]*

KEYWORDS. Collection development, collections cooperation, Janus Conference, Ross Atkinson, digital resources, analog resources, collections models, research libraries, library competition, library status

Dan Hazen is Associate Librarian of Harvard College for Collection Development, Harvard University Libraries, Office of the Librarian, Room 110, Harvard Yard, Cambridge, MA 02138 (E-mail: dchazen@fas.harvard.edu).

[Haworth co-indexing entry note]: "The Cooperative Conundrum in the Digital Age." Hazen, Dan. Co-published simultaneously in *Journal of Library Administration* (The Haworth Information Press, an imprint of The Haworth Press, Inc.) Vol. 46, No. 2, 2007, pp. 101-118; and: *Print vs. Digital: The Future of Coexistence* (ed: Sul H. Lee) The Haworth Information Press, an imprint of The Haworth Press, Inc., 2007, pp. 101-118. Single or multiple copies of this article are available for a fee from The Haworth Document Delivery Service [1-800-HAWORTH, 9:00 a.m. - 5:00 p.m. (EST). E-mail address: docdelivery@haworthpress.com].

INTRODUCTION

The language that we use to discuss library collections, the information marketplace, and cooperative action has its roots in the analog era. Much of the narrative, and many of its markers, remain both relevant and essential. But we may find that our rhetoric also limits our perceptions as we move into a digital environment. Several initiatives, involving on-the-ground activity as well as conceptual work, embody new approaches. The cooperative arena is particularly ripe for change.

This essay opens by reviewing some salient features of library cooperation as it has been pursued in the past. Four aspects of our emerging environment are then described at greater length. Two of these–an initial questioning of the relationship between de facto systems and explicit cooperation, and a revised conceptual framework for library collections–focus on the mental models with which we structure our activities. Two others focus on more practical issues, one by describing a fledgling yet potentially transformative collective endeavor among research libraries as a group, and the second by beginning to explore some of the deep-seated divisions within and around this community.

Collections cooperation in the analog world has pursued shared access to tangible information objects, mostly books, microfilms, and journals, that are held in limited quantity and are available–necessarily–with delay. The basic functions include identifying these typically low use and/or high-priced resources; acquiring them for library collections; describing them so that students, scholars, and librarian intermediaries can locate them; and delivering them to users. Arrangements for governance and sustainability, while essential as well, are not always explicit.

Two main models for cooperation have prevailed within this resolutely material universe. The first is based on distributed collections, functions, and costs. Bilateral arrangements, for example, those between Duke and the University of North Carolina, or Stanford and Berkeley, are effective and also easy to understand. Each partner assumes primary responsibility for certain collections areas, with shared access to the results. Similar yet more extensive initiatives, say the Farmington Plan or the Conspectus effort, have required more complex acquisitions agreements, governance, and infrastructure. All these programs can energize familiar local behaviors, for instance by reinforcing bibliographers' collecting obsessions within carefully delimited domains. Local autonomy is thereby framed within cooperative responsibilities.

A second model entails central collections and infrastructure, sustained through shared funding and governance, that draw forth efficiencies of scale and specialized capacities in support of a dispersed user community. The Center for Research Libraries epitomizes this approach, as do its affiliated Area Studies Microform Projects. The model again presumes that scarce, low-use resources can most effectively be handled through structured arrangements on behalf of a larger group.

A third variant seeks first to create or consolidate a resource of potential community interest, and then to construct an audience. A great deal of commercial microfilming, for instance, has relied on up-front investments to assemble sets of materials that were sometimes scattered as well as scarce or unique. The instantly "canonical" arrays of primary sources thus created have then become broadly available for purchase. Libraries and consortia have sometimes taken the same approach.

These kinds of initiatives have entailed prodigious efforts and immense enthusiasm. Assessments of results, however, are often ambivalent. It's routine to praise the achievements of the Center for Research Libraries, bilateral agreements, and some cooperative experiments. Large microfilm sets have fostered access to resources that would otherwise be unavailable. However, cost and benefit calculations are seldom straightforward, and sustainability is frequently an open question. Projects that privatize and commercialize the public domain raise doubts of their own.

Other skeptical evaluations look at what our cooperative efforts have not managed to achieve. These analyses, taken together, are somewhat bipolar. On one hand, common wisdom has it that our library collections are massively duplicative, with too many materials then receiving very little use. Well-designed cooperation would minimize this redundancy. Conversely, some early comparative collections assessments based on OCLC's massive bibliographic database signal a wide distribution of unique holdings. This in turn suggests a huge, unrecognized common agenda of devising cost-effective means to preserve, share, and collectively care for an underappreciated community resource. Both arguments indicate that we still lack an adequate analysis of when and how hardcopy cooperation can work.

Thus, briefly, our (continuing) hardcopy past. And again we ask where we've gotten with cooperation, and where we may be going. This inquiry by now includes several interwoven threads. One concerns the very nature of cooperation. Does this activity have to be explicit? To what extent do academic and research libraries already function as a de facto integrated system, regardless of any formal understandings? How does competition among the colleges and universities within which most research libraries are embedded (and, indeed, among the libraries themselves) shape our cooperative inclinations? And how do commercial offerings affect our cross-institutional efforts as they structure the information universe and variously inhibit, or stimulate, a coordinated response?

Second, and after some twenty years of often overheated rhetoric, a predominantly digital information universe is finally becoming the norm for many aspects of post-secondary education. Numerous retrospective digitizing projects, plus the growing array of current digital resources, are changing the information and library landscapes. But we've been slow to develop fully coherent responses–perhaps because we have so far managed to somehow muddle along, perhaps because the technologies have so rapidly evolved, perhaps because today's overlays of intellectual property regimes and rights management structures remain so unfriendly and complex. Only now are we documenting what's been done in the virtual arena; controlling redundancy; articulating a common set of digital priorities; and revamping our services in light of scholarly imperatives, technological possibility, legal constraints, and user expectations.

A third broad concern is illuminated by mass digitization efforts, including Google's large-scale projects. Commercial content providers have, to no one's surprise, structured a market that first and foremost meets their own needs. It's time, and perhaps past time, to see whether the library community can lead as well as simply react to these shifts. The "Janus Conference on Research Library Collections," held at Cornell in the fall of 2005, launched one such exercise. The first of its two central themes involves our current conceptual framework for collection development. This structure was articulated about thirty years ago, when information was conveyed via print publications and libraries were just starting to automate their catalogs. The world has changed, and our models need to adjust.

But the Janus Conference aspired to practical action as well. Libraries are still grinding through the awkward and expensive shift from an entirely analog environment toward an overwhelmingly digital universe. The range, requirements, and potential of virtual information are different from those of their hard-copy predecessors. Our organizations, budgets, and procedures tend to separately address the two realms, inflating our costs and reducing our efficiency. How can we accelerate and shape the digital transition?

A fourth broad concern, finally, assesses whether new perceptions of our information context and institutional goals imply specialized roles for different institutions. Our increasingly creaky criteria for library success, epitomized in the ARL rankings, have enforced an intractable preoccupation with volume counts and size. We are beginning to acknowledge that achievement can take many forms, suggesting a multidimensional evaluative mosaic. Just within the collections realm, everyone understands the relentless erosion of libraries' purchasing power: many institutions are by now extremely limited in what they can acquire. But we have hesitated to take the next step by talking openly about which libraries, organizations, informal groupings, and (perhaps) external agencies will most effectively take the lead in addressing particular challenges relating to collections and information.

Each of these four broad themes invites discussion and debate. Each could support its own array of conferences and ancillary arrangements for communication, consensus-building, and action. This essay only begins to suggest some possibilities.

LIBRARIES AND SYSTEMS

Let us consider ants. Any particular ant, one imagines, wakes up in the morning and launches into its daily routine as an autonomous creature, albeit one whose behaviors are deeply embedded within a complex social structure. Entomologists, of course, look at ants and see colonies and groups, not discrete individuals. The contrasting perspectives of actors and observers support radically different conclusions concerning both behavior and possibility. Similar characterizations apply elsewhere in the animal world, say to bees or guppies or flocking birds, and perhaps well beyond. What of our libraries? Do they fall along their own spectrum that spans a range from self-defined individualism on one end, to communal patternings on the other?

Ant-thropomorphism aside, we have yet to adequately analyze libraries as comprising a system as well as standing in atomistic isolation, or even as semi-social organizations whose connections go beyond conscious cooperative programs. If and as we seek this perspective, questions of agency are impossible to avoid. Can a system be purposeful, or even coherent, if no one is in charge? Is there a bibliothecal counterpart to the "invisible hand" of classical economics? Looking to the future, can we escape the intensive work of identifying constituencies and teasing out the political dimensions of a "library project" through which we together confront and create our environment?

Libraries, each unique in its origins and sovereign in its finances, jointly comprise a de facto network. Most of our institutions adhere to common standards and practices. Shared bibliographic databases and, increasingly, metadata harvesting and discovery tools, reflect a higher degree of coherence.[1] (Sophisticated search engines may foster a similar appearance, albeit from a more haphazard base and in a less certain way.) Interoperable systems provide a functional foundation for concerted cooperative action. But further movement toward a fully integrated and deliberately interdependent system assumes administration and overhead–in a word, bureaucracy. Is a high level of articulation something we need consciously to pursue? Is the end state desirable, or simply inevitable?

Another way to perceive this progression focuses on interlocking feedback loops of user needs, service improvements, and operational capabilities. Standardized bibliographic control, for example, traces back to common cataloging codes and classification systems, tools like the *National Union Catalog*, and then such automated bibliographic databases as OCLC and RLIN. Interlibrary loan and systematic resource sharing have followed in this wake, engendering their own logic (albeit somewhat spottier of a practice) of specialized collecting and planned interdependence.

Local experiences of overstuffed stacks and reliance on remote storage have, perhaps inadvertently, bolstered the case for conscious coordination. Almost all libraries point to on-site holdings that are readily accessible. Other materials may be in remote storage, with retrieval typically delayed by a day or two. Some multi-library consortia offer expedited interlibrary loan in about the same length of time. The growing trend toward digital document delivery likewise simplifies quick access to offsite materials. Whether anticipated or not, new interdependencies and also synergies routinely emerge as remote materials come within reach. These systems, whether spontaneous or planned, beg for closer analysis.

MODELS FOR COLLECTIONS AND COOPERATION

Collections

Our vocabularies and frameworks for collection development were constructed when hardcopy transactions were the only available option.

The information world turned on local holdings, with resource sharing playing a decidedly secondary role. The Conspectus initiative of the 1980s, arguably the community's most ambitious recent effort, reflected the same perspective.[2] We need to rethink our conceptual framework for today's academic library collections, and then how this may affect the cooperative arena.

Our library resources, whether analog or digital, and whether viewed individually or collectively, fall into four broad "ideal" categories. To begin with, all academic libraries support instruction. They thus provide basic bibliographies and reference works, reading list materials, and the core sources fundamental to the disciplines and fields taught in each parent institution. The function is ubiquitous, and understandings of a particular field's core resources tend to carry across from place to place.

Second, academic libraries in institutions that support faculty research or advanced study seek to capture some or all of the record of scholarship. This rubric includes the published outputs of colleges and universities, commercial laboratories and trade organizations, think tanks and scholarly societies, academies and associations, specialized agencies and ad hoc research groups. An institution's appetite may vary within this large realm–only American university press publications, perhaps; or a multinational, multilingual sampler; or (in aspiration even if not actuality) exhaustive coverage. These holdings, which recapitulate and chronicle the scholarly record, sustain the ongoing, cumulative process of creating new knowledge.

An immense third category comprises all organized human expression, or the full range of primary sources. These are the raw materials for future scholarship, and their nature has become ever more eclectic. Libraries have always acquired a broad representation of creative literature–novels, drama, poetry, and the like. Selective but significant arrays of local and international newspapers, and of government documents, are enduring mainstays as well. Some collections of particular note have been constructed around the wholesale acquisition of specialized private libraries. Other primary sources have only more recently been acknowledged within the scholarly mainstream. Ephemera and gray literature, pamphlets, popular magazines, visual images and photographs, films and video, manuscripts and archival collections, and sound recordings are all by now considered essential. Digital resources, structured datasets, and web-based products likewise demand attention.

Unorganized raw data, finally, comprise a category of information with which we're only beginning to grapple. Scholars' research notes–unruly file cabinets, boxes of scribbles and scrawls–provide a simple example. Hardcopy data generated in the course of experiments, surveys, and observations are similar. Today's masses of e-mail communications, blogs and chatrooms, digital satellite imagery, remote sensing data, raw survey responses, meteorological measurements, and the like, present challenges of capture and curation that we have barely begun to address.[3]

Scholarship and teaching draw upon different blends of these four categories between one discipline and the next. The variations are especially pronounced for primary resources. Research in history or cultural studies typically draws upon an encompassing array of original documents and materials. Scholarship in some other humanistic fields, for example philosophy, is often more narrowly framed. But the ground is also shifting, for instance as classical scholarship broadens beyond a confined documentary canon to include material culture and archeological evidence. Conversely, it's commonplace to assert that the library is the humanist's laboratory, implying that scientific research relies less substantially on the written record. Here, too, we need a more nuanced understanding. Historic field surveys are essential for botanical and zoological research. So, for astronomers, are celestial observations from both past and present. Scholars' need for non-current literature in disciplines like chemistry or physics, by contrast, does for now seem more limited.

The information resources needed to support teaching and scholarship in specific fields vary in shifting and sometimes unexpected ways. Furthermore, our four collections categories are by no means rigid. Thus, for example, today's pedagogical models routinely require students to grapple with primary sources as well as synthetic texts. The consequent mingling can complicate close-grained collections planning. By expanding the universe of potentially relevant materials, it also reinforces the case for cooperation.

In sum: many disciplines look to broader arrays of research resources than they have in the past. Today's pedagogical models engage learners with primary sources as well as textbooks and summaries. More and more information is available in digital formats, with their complex legal and economic ramifications. These shifts make it increasingly difficult to interpret and manage collections needs solely from within our institutions.

Cooperation

Library budgets and collections are under pressure. Some academic libraries are by now pretty much limited to providing only curricular support. We are also changing our definitions of library success, paying particular attention to aggressive service models associated with focused teaching and learning. New instruments to assess measurable outcomes and user satisfaction, LibQUAL™ and the like, are another manifestation of change. All these shifts comprise a necessary corrective to the profession's longstanding preoccupation with collection size. This re-centered perspective also reflects that our collections are no longer what they've been.

Digital resources further affect both the information universe and our perceptions of libraries in system. We've gradually become adept at understanding, documenting, and managing digital objects. Metadata schemas and harvesting tools, format registries, standardized software, and insistent anxiety around preservation, are all nudging the digital cosmos toward predictability and control. Our legal regime has lagged, but even here the interplay among user needs, legislative mandate, and commercial imperative may produce workable accommodations. Open access resources, institutional and disciplinary repositories, and new models for scholarly communication are part of the same picture.

Digital information stands to alter cooperative collection development in several different ways. The commonplace recognition that e-resources are available without regard to a user's geographic location is one cornerstone for enhanced cooperative efforts: the need to store and transport physical objects has vanished. (Questions of long-term preservation and stewardship of course still remain.) The nature of consortia has been similarly liberated as geography becomes less relevant, though convincing new models have not yet emerged. The current roster of high-use digital products has by and large been framed and then created by single-source providers, the profit-driven Elseviers on one hand, the non-profit JSTORs on the other. Our widely dispersed consumer community may generate equally significant results. Production, and not just consumption or funding, can become a distributed function within the virtual environment.[4] We have the means to cooperatively create and structure more encompassing digital collections, and our economic constraints reinforce this approach. It's time to act.

Finally, digital reformatting allows added-value activities not feasible in the analog age, when fairly simple tasks like assembling microfilm sets out of several source collections were about all we could manage. Electronic products lend themselves to such enhancements as full-text searchability, marked-up content, and links to related resources. The systems that will allow us to minimize inadvertent duplication, and the repository infrastructure required for long-term digital archiving, are not fully in place.

While digital products could be universally accessible, actual use is typically constrained by license terms and prices. Efforts to re-ground the process of scholarly communication are still incipient. They are also probably most appropriately managed, with library participation, at other levels of our institutions. Libraries have instead focused on formal and informal consortia to leverage our aggregated purchasing power—basically buyers' clubs. One can certainly imagine an alternative world in which a unified library community approaches information providers as equals, or even sets the terms by which vendors can address the information needs that we define.[5]

Collective action may allow us to more fully shape both the landscape and the marketplace for electronic resources. The traditional cooperative emphasis on the expensive, obscure, low-demand resources that we can share without inconveniencing local users might be turned on its head as we together identify and digitally address core materials. Cooperative activities in the digital realm can also cut across and encompass all four categories of collection resources. Plans for a national cyberinfrastructure, for example, particularly emphasize the realm of raw data. These categories will also continue to blur around the edges. The structures to achieve these digital visions, however, are not now in place.

THE JANUS CONFERENCE

Cornell University's long-term Collection Development Officer, Ross Atkinson, for decades helped guide the research library community toward fuller understandings of library collections and how they could be most effective.[6] Atkinson was the driving force behind a fall 2005 meeting in Ithaca entitled "The Janus Conference on Research Library Collections: Managing the Shifting Ground Between Writers and Readers." This meeting had two main goals: to update our conceptual framework for library collections; and to implement practical measures to better position academic libraries within the realm of scholarly communication, in order to improve their services to our students and scholars.

These goals were addressed at Cornell by a group of perhaps seventy collection development administrators, and others. The central debate built from three commissioned papers that considered our emerging digital realm from as many different perspectives. Mark Dimunation, from the Library of Congress, emphasized the enduring and unique value of original artifacts–books, manuscripts, maps, and on–whatever the attractions of digital surrogates. The sensory attributes and sensual substance of our cultural heritage convey messages in and of themselves. Mark Sandler, from the University of Michigan, followed with an economics-inflected analysis of the digital realm, its premises and also some of its pitfalls. The "long tail" effect of unconstrained electronic storage space and discovery capacity, customized offerings tailored to niche markets, carefully structured tiers of added value, individualized service options, and on, all offer a subtle and largely encouraging sense of how scholarly resources might evolve. The Université de Montréal's Jean-Claude Guédon, finally, spoke to the complex interrelationships among readers and texts. This delicate and typically contingent interplay stands to be energized in potentially transformative ways as the virtual world engages new combinations of readers and writers who are at once co-participants and co-creators. The digital world challenges and empowers us in ways fundamentally different from what we have known.

These papers formed the backdrop for the meeting's core work. Ross Atkinson confronted the group with the argument that scholarly communication, the information marketplace, and academic libraries are moving inexorably toward an overwhelmingly digital future. Our transition costs, as we sustain dual systems for analog and digital information, are immense. Moreover, we are following rather than directing the process. The lack of a coherent, shared strategy limits our ability to shape the new landscape. To that same degree, we have abandoned some of our core responsibilities vis-à-vis the academic community. How can research libraries together mobilize to take charge of change?

The beginnings of an action plan were framed through six deliberatively provocative challenges to the group. Each was presented as a general proposition, followed by a possible scenario for action:[7]

1. *RECON.* Convert to digital form objects currently only available in traditional form.

   Action for Consideration: Each research library will transfer 10% of its materials budget annually to a central fund, to be used for mass digitization. Decisions on what to digitize in what order will be made by a committee of research library collection development officers, special collections managers, and technical specialists.

2. *PROCON.* Ensure objects published in the future are available in digital form.

   Action for Consideration: Subsequent to 1 January 2008, research libraries will no longer purchase materials published in North America or Western Europe that are not in digital form.

3. *Core Definition.* Define collectively the notification objects that compose a core collection in each discipline.

   Action for Consideration: Building of separate, local collections of basic level materials (2+ level) will be discontinued in research libraries. Instead, committees of subject specialists (operating primarily online) will agree upon what belongs in a basic or core collection, and all research libraries with at least a basic collection in the subject will automatically acquire those materials.

4. *Publisher Relations.* Negotiate collectively with publishers on the best possible access to notification sources.

   Action for Consideration: Research libraries will agree upon fair price ceilings for all types of notification sources, and will further agree to buy no materials that exceed these ceilings.

5. *Archiving.* Ensure the coordinated, long-term maintenance of traditional and digital holdings.

   Action for Consideration: With the exception of clearly defined special collections materials, all print materials published between 1830 and 1960 should be transferred to a regional print repository (constructed, if necessary, for that purpose). Each regional repository should sell or discard any duplicates it receives that are available in other repositories (so that it retains only one copy). At the same time, all digital objects selected by all research libraries should be added to an OAIS-based repository that can meet the certification requirements as defined by RLG/NARA.

6. *Alternative Channels for Scholarly Communication.* Create a network of publishing structures that scholars can use as a supplement or alternative to standard scholarly publishing channels.

   Action for Consideration: Research libraries will agree on the design and services of an open access repository. Each research library will select a subject, and, working with local faculty and other appropriate stakeholders, such as scholarly societies, will create an open access repository for that subject, using funding from the materials budget. Supporting the repository will be the materials budget's highest priority.

Participants were randomly assigned to working groups that spent several hours discussing whether and how "their" challenge might be addressed—with some time to consider the other challenges as well. Most groups reported a similar sequence of initial skepticism, focused on problematic terms and aggressive phraseology. But the discussions then gradually moved away from these specifics in a process that resulted in overall group support for most of the general principles behind each proposition. Tellingly, those groups that could consider other challenges tended to replicate the same rather hesitant sequence, usually without enough time to move beyond the initial doubts.

All the group responses were melded together for presentation to the plenary. The contrast between usually positive reactions from each group that "owned" a particular challenge, and other groups' more skeptical assessments, came into sharp relief as the relatively conservative amalgamated opinions evoked spirited dissent from the original "owning" groups. The conference thus swung from radical initial scenarios to watered down overall reactions, with the groups most fully immersed in each challenge most supportive of change; and then to late-day push-back toward a more adventuresome stance. The session ended as self-selected working groups agreed to refine each challenge and suggest action steps as well.

The reworked proposals were then presented for further discussion at the Chief Collection Development Officers session at ALA's Midwinter meeting in January, 2006. These exchanges allowed additional clarifications, and also community suggestions for practical measures to advance each "challenge" area. A still-jelling coordinating structure was also established in order to shepherd along the entire process. An emerging sense of priorities among the challenges, and logical sequences for implementation, likewise took shape.

As of the spring of 2006, all six of the original challenges had assumed a new (and lengthier) form on the Janus Conference website. The conversations continue: these versions remain works in progress. Concrete action plans are emerging as well. A few examples of the revised proposals will suggest where things stand:

> *Challenge 1, RECON.* Converting the scholarly record. Collection development and other interested librarians from academic and re-search libraries will create a working group to develop and begin implementing a plan for a national mass digitization project to convert holdings in North American research libraries.
>
> The group will accomplish the following:
>
> - recommend a structure for administering and coordinating the proj-ect that ensures active support from institutions and associations whose backing will be necessary for the success of the project.
> - recommend selection models and best practices for the initial stages of the project that will demonstrate its value, importance and viability.
> - while actively seeking grant support to begin the work of the project, assume that the research library community must de-vote substantial resources, financial and human, to the project and be the primary source of funding.
> - take into account projects already in place nationally and inter-nationally, and involve participants in those projects in planning this more global effort.
>
> *Challenge 2, PROCON.* Ensuring future publications are in digital form. Research libraries are committed to moving to an environ-ment in the medium term future (e.g., by the end of the decade), in which most newly published materials are acquired in digital form. Research libraries will work with scholars, publishers, and each other in order to achieve this. Research libraries agree to shift to e-only by 2008 for those publications that are available in both print and electronic form including: journals, reference books, textbooks, government documents and other areas like electronic books as the electronic publishing models develop. A complete transition to digital form by 2008 is dependent on the existence of trusted archives for digital content.
>
> *Challenge 4, Licensing Principles* (formerly Publisher Relations). Negotiate collectively with publishers on the best possible access

to e-content. Research libraries will make every effort to sign no licenses that include non-disclosure clauses, and to share among themselves the terms of agreements with all publishers. Public universities shall publicly post licenses and business terms on their Web sites. Research libraries will make every effort to ensure that licenses include such options as the right to use publications with course management software, the right to use publications for e-reserve, the right to fulfill ILL requests according to existing ILL guidelines and the right of authors to retain copyright and make their publications available in open access repositories or other archives. Research libraries will make every effort to ensure that licenses include provisions for perpetual access and archival deposit of licensed content.

In general terms, progress on the "Archiving" challenge is perceived as a precondition for any other measure that would increase our reliance upon digital objects. The notion of a national approval plan to provide the core literature needed by many libraries, and the degree to which we might be ambitious in reshaping publisher relations and licensing terms, remain under very active discussion. At least two broad obstacles also remain. Janus participants themselves, and others who have only heard of the conference and its proposals, are divided over both the process and the proposals. Framing the initial challenges in terms of highly prescriptive mandates managed by a small inner circle–some conjure up a "librarians' soviet"–may have been threatening as well as provocative. On a different level, all the Janus participants have returned to work lives filled with everyday pressures and distractions. The ongoing commitments required to achieve timely outcomes are by no means assured.[8]

CASTE MENTALITIES AND DIVISIONS OF LABOR

The Janus exercise would mobilize academic libraries in the joint pursuit of common goals. It therefore both assumes and presumes to strengthen a systemic perspective. Some of the conference challenges also focus on particular categories within our four-tiered model for library collections and the information landscape. A shared approval plan for "core materials," for example, would focus on the resources that provide curricular support. The overall Janus emphasis on concerted cooperative action, however, may underplay the complementary need to carefully distinguish among the roles and possibilities of the cooperating libraries. Both familiar and less obvious elements may here be in play. Continuing shifts in scholarly communication and the information marketplace likewise affect the analysis.

We typically, albeit rather ambivalently, acknowledge that a few "libraries of last resort" carry our heaviest collections load. The list includes the two dozen or so libraries at the top of the ARL rankings, plus a few others like the Library of Congress and the New York Public Library. These very large academic libraries are like all others in providing core resources and curricular support. They also seek very full representations of the scholarly record. And they pursue generous (though inevitably limited) segments of primary resources or "recorded human expression."

Many other libraries aspire to collections that encompass the same variety of curricular support, the scholarly record, and primary resources. Strong holdings of local publications are common fixtures of both public and academic libraries, and unique special collections can turn up anywhere. Early results from OCLC's collection analysis service seem to suggest a wide scattering of unique materials among many libraries.[9] One-of-a-kind holdings are everywhere sources of pride and evidence of distinction. Ensuring appropriate arrangements for stewardship may be more difficult, and identifying those libraries whose unique holdings make them de facto centerpieces for coordinated activity is complicated in both political and operational terms.

The picture becomes more complex from a global perspective. North American libraries form one implicit system. Yet this system is complemented and often overshadowed by overseas repositories. Whether the focus is massive national libraries or modest municipal collections, these non-North American institutions provide unparalleled local coverage—even in cases where straitened budgets may preclude their full participation in the developed world's information marketplace. Large-scale cooperation needs to welcome these libraries into ethical and equitable partnerships that consciously address a range of digital and hardcopy collecting capabilities.

Another challenge reflects the increasingly blurred boundaries among different categories of cultural artifacts. Researchers use materials associated with all manner of custodial agencies, both formal and informal. Search engines likewise cut across informational and also institutional domains. Our careful distinctions between libraries, archives, and museums thus carry less and less meaning. Dividing lines between private collections and public repositories are often becoming less relevant as well.

Some of the issues at first blush seem to involve bragging rights: who's biggest, who's best, who's most worthy. They also carry fiscal overtones. The largest libraries and museums, those that have built the most massive collections, are typically presumed affluent. Even when this is true, is it realistic to expect these institutions to finance long-term preservation and digitization on their own, as a disinterested community service? If more broad-based support is in order, how will it be arranged? What role do cooperative entities like the Center for Research Libraries have to play? If libraries fail to act, will commercial players fill the void? Where will we then stand, if others can more effectively mediate between users and information? The questions significantly outnumber our answers.

CONCLUSION

The language that we use in some respects creates our reality. While the words and concepts with which we describe library collections and cooperation come from the recent past, that past is also very different from the world of today. Its underlying assumptions include free-standing collections of tangible objects within autonomous institutions, for which responses to environmental, programmatic, and marketplace challenges are pretty much a local concern. We now need to adjust our thinking, looking realistically to see where we can together have a greater impact and how we can most effectively create change. We also need to act, to complement our rhetoric with work, and to buttress our narratives with concrete steps and planned behaviors.

NOTES

1. A recent catalog of standards and best practices driven primarily by technology is found in Peter Webster, "Interconnected and Innovative Libraries: Factors Tying Libraries More Closely Together," *Library Trends* 54-3 (Winter 2006), pp. 382-393. (Issue title: "Library Resource Sharing Networks.")

2. Newer and very promising cooperative experiments have tended to build backward from efficient arrangements for document delivery and interlibrary loan, into the collections realm. Both OhioLINK and Borrow Direct suggest some of the possibilities.

3. See, for example, *Revolutionizing Science and Engineering Through Cyber-infrastructure: Report of the National Science Foundation Blue-Ribbon Advisory Panel on Cyberinfrastructure* (2003) http://dlist.sir.arizona.edu/897/, and *The Draft Report of the American Council of Learned Societies' Commission on Cyberinfra-structure for Humanities and Social Sciences (for public comment)* (2005) http://acls.org/cyberinfrastructure/acls-ci-public.pdf.

4. American Memory (http://memory.loc.gov/ammem/index.html), for example, includes separate collections from a number of institutions, so far joined together more as a patchwork than in a seamless cross-searchable aggregation.

5. See the Center for Research Libraries *Request for Information: Joint Venture for the Cooperative Digitization and Dissemination of World Newspapers* (April 18, 2006).

6. Following an extended illness, Ross Atkinson passed away early in March, 2006. He is missed.

7. A complete set of conference-related information, including webcasts of the proceedings, is available on the Janus website: http://janusconference.library.cornell.edu/. The jargon in some of the original challenges echoes the terminology of the Conspectus iniitative, and also Ross Atkinson's collections vocabulary.

8. These assessments are current as of April, 2006. The conversation continues to unfold, sometimes quite quickly.

9. Early collections comparisons using the OCLC Collections Analysis tool reflect a database that still underrepresents the holdings of many institutions. Several large-scale dataloads will increase its accuracy in reflecting overall coverage. Careful sampling studies are then needed in order to verify the possible extent of overlapping or duplicative records that could also distort assessment results.

doi:10.1300/J111v46n02_08

The End of Print Journals: (In)Frequently Asked Questions

Karen Hunter

SUMMARY. Scholarly journals have been moving from paper only to paper plus electronic versions. Cessation of the paper version requires satisfying diverse needs of librarians, university administrators, authors, readers, and publishers. doi:10.1300/J111v46n02_09 *[Article copies available for a fee from The Haworth Document Delivery Service: 1-800-HAWORTH. E-mail address: <docdelivery@haworthpress.com> Website: <http://www.HaworthPress.com> © 2007 by The Haworth Press, Inc. All rights reserved.]*

KEYWORDS. Serials, journals, digital archiving, digital preservation, scholarly publishing, electronic journals

For 341 years–since their beginnings in 1665–scientific journals have been distributed to their readers in print. For the last decade electronic delivery has grown alongside print and has now overtaken print as the preferred medium of access, if not actual reading. For library and

---

Karen Hunter is Senior Vice President, Elsevier, 360 Park Avenue South, New York, NY 10010 (E-mail: k.hunter@elsevier.com).

Paper delivered at the University of Oklahoma Conference "Printed Resources and Digital Information: The Future of Coexistence," March 2-3, 2006, Oklahoma City, OK.

[Haworth co-indexing entry note]: "The End of Print Journals: (In)Frequently Asked Questions." Hunter, Karen. Co-published simultaneously in *Journal of Library Administration* (The Haworth Information Press, an imprint of The Haworth Press, Inc.) Vol. 46, No. 2, 2007, pp. 119-132; and: *Print vs. Digital: The Future of Coexistence* (ed: Sul H. Lee) The Haworth Information Press, an imprint of The Haworth Press, Inc., 2007, pp. 119-132. Single or multiple copies of this article are available for a fee from The Haworth Document Delivery Service [1-800-HAWORTH, 9:00 a.m. - 5:00 p.m. (EST). E-mail address: docdelivery@haworthpress.com].

other institutional subscribers, the conversion to e-only subscriptions is no longer the bold and risky move it was five years ago. For Elsevier, nearly 40% of our ScienceDirect™ subscription revenues are e-only, in some cases supplemented by paper subscriptions to a few titles. This results in some direct library savings on both the subscription price (when compared with print plus electronic) and on check-in, shelving, binding, and space. As publishers increasingly digitize their backfiles, library's real estate savings increase as bound back volumes can be gradually moved to an off-campus storage facility.

In this environment it seems natural, therefore, to assume that journal publishers must already be planning for an end to the production of the printed paper issues of the journals. (And the vast majority of the 20,000+ peer reviewed journals have print editions.) Surely, publishers must have a schedule in mind for this. But, in fact, that plan is not in place among the major journal publishers. When asked whether an end to print was in their plans, my publishing colleagues and competitors have said they have no date in mind. But, at the same time, I have heard from both university administrators and librarians that from their perspective it *is* time for publishers to make serious plans for the end of print.

All of which led me to this presentation, which is an attempt to identify the issues that would have to be resolved to make going e-only–no print edition–a viable publisher option for existing print journals. In considering this, I will address four points:

- first, the concerns of librarians and institutional administrators;
- second, the perspectives of authors and readers;
- third, the issues that publishers wrestle with; and
- fourth, as the need for persistent digital archiving is a critical element that runs through all stakeholders' interests, I will take a more detailed look at archiving today.

LIBRARIANS AND INSTITUTIONAL ADMINISTRATORS

The principal motivation for librarians and administrators in advocating an end to print is cost-savings. Fifteen to twenty years ago, when electronic journal distribution was but an early gleam in our eyes, many librarians expected that there would be a dramatic reduction in subscription cost for existing paper journals when electronic alternatives would be available. That expectation was grounded primarily in a misunderstanding of journal economics (an over-allocation of the costs that are attributable to printing and mailing of a single issue to a single sub-scriber). Until a publisher can completely abandon printing, there are few costs to be saved on the typical short-run academic journal by re-ducing the print run from, for example, 1,000 to 800 copies, and putting 200 fewer copies in the mail. I was once told, probably apocryphally, that on some journals more paper was used getting the press set up than in the printing itself. In any case, it did not take long for librarians to understand that this was regrettably wishful thinking. Indeed, with the prevailing print plus electronic model, the cost of the subscription in-creased and the support costs also rose, as new activities (such as the ne-gotiation and administration of licenses) were added. What can be gained by a library deciding to cancel print and go electronic only is a discount of perhaps 10% in the list subscription price, but not sweeping savings.

The result is an increasing belief among librarians that the transi-tional period of supporting two media for the same information has to end as quickly as possible. Our library advisors are now saying that we should be actively planning to end print. The same message is coming from some provosts and other university administrators and it is based, again, on cost concerns. There is a strong desire to reduce the need for continuing investment in buildings.

One might ask: why does the publisher need to stop printing paper copies when the individual library can make the decision–which hun-dreds have–to stop ordering the paper and order electronic-only? Why throw out the baby with the bathwater? Just make the e-only decision for your library and all is well. You save check-in, shelving, reshelving, binding and the cost of the shelves themselves, the bricks and mortar, the heat, light and insurance, etc. You can sleep at night assured that you have made the right move and that there is nothing to be concerned about.

Unfortunately, it doesn't seem to quite work that way for all librari-ans and here I have to speculate (although my view has been confirmed in informal research). My hypothesis is as follows: So long as there is both a print and an electronic edition of a journal, the community will view the print as the definitive edition and be concerned that the elec-tronic edition may not totally match the print, hence the need for some-one to maintain the print. Librarians will only be *really* comfortable going electronic-only when there is no print edition for comparison.

This is, of course, not the only concern of librarians. Over the past three-to-four years librarians have dealt with other issues, including:

- In a world in which libraries license rather than own e-journals, what rights do they have for permanent access to the material paid for, particularly when the library stops subscribing? This is still an evolving area and varies by publisher and has strong emotional attributes. For example, from the beginning of its ScienceDirect service, Elsevier has given its subscribers the option to host it locally or, if using the Web online service, to receive copies of the files upon cancellation. While one would think this would provide the necessary reassurance–you can always take possession–it has not been enough. We have added the right, even if you totally stop being a ScienceDirect licensee, to continue accessing the ScienceDirect online service for access to previously subscribed material. As Elsevier has real costs to provide this service, those costs are passed on to the former customer. And that fee, lowered twice, is still fought. While in the 1980s and 1990s access to electronic bibliographic databases never generated calls for ownership or perpetual access after cancellation, with journals there are clearly notions of entitlement that tie to the print model.
- Will faculty accept e-only? From what I am told, the answer is "yes," but clearly this is not black and white for all faculty in all disciplines.
- Will students and faculty still come to the library? Faculty perhaps not, students yes, but for other reasons–a redefinition of the library as place and "place as library." This change has already happened for journals–desktop access has replaced the trip to the library–and stopping print will make little difference.
- What will be the role of the library and librarians with journals? Again, this is not print related. Librarians play many roles with respect to journals, including the continuing role of financial guardian, selector and acquirer, re-enforced through online branding of the library as the source of the service; integrator into seamless, easily-used discovery and access systems; educator on the differentiation of peer-reviewed literature from non-certified material uncovered in a Web (Google) search.
- What is the role of subscription agents in an e-only world? Unclear and this will, indeed, be further complicated when print ends.
- How will this affect pricing models? Are we still in a title-by-title subscription mode or something else more like a database? Pricing models are evolving anyway and are not necessarily dependent on what happens to print.

University provosts and other administrators have an overlapping list of concerns. They are also looking at faculty (and student) acceptance and at capital cost implications. They may want assurance of a sensitivity to differences by discipline, such that a broad decision with respect to going e-only for a multi-disciplinary publisher doesn't result in some disciplines feeling their needs have not been considered adequately. They will have to deal with how to allocate budgets: if there are real savings in the library, will the library benefit from it (and have money to spend on other things) or will that money go to other campus needs and demands?

Finally, common to both librarians and administrators is the core concern about continued access in the future. This takes two forms: the previously-mentioned perpetual access to that which has been licensed and permanent research community access to the journal literature across time–to preserve and continue to certify the work of today's research authors and to ensure the literature's persistence and availability for future researchers' use. What happens when the publisher withdraws an electronic work from online access, or goes out of business, or otherwise makes access impossible? And who assures that the files will be physically useable? Who will pay for this? Proper digital preservation–preservation that is sustainable as to policy, technology, and economics–is the sine qua non in the discussion of the end of print. If digital archiving has not been put in place such that all parts of the community are satisfied that the future is as secure as it can be at this time, we cannot proceed. But I will return to this later.

AUTHORS AND READERS

Authors share the archival concerns of librarians and provosts: will my work be available forever? They also may have concern about who has access to their work. At one time this would have been a question of whether there are as many people having access to electronic editions as to the paper version. It is difficult to imagine such a discussion today. Consider that in the case of Elsevier's ScienceDirect there are over 10 million researchers and students with immediate desktop access. Contrast that with the in-library access in a paper-only world where there were perhaps 300 or 1,200 copies to be accessed in the entire international research community.

The more relevant question is: are there researchers who have no e-access? Perhaps some, but I would argue two things:

- First, there are more researchers in the developed world with electronic access than with print access. If you look just at the Elsevier figures for the UK as an example, over 90% of all researchers have desktop access to all Elsevier journals electronically. That level of access and efficiency was certainly not the case with paper only. Authors' visibility is extraordinarily greater in an electronic world.
- Second, electronic access via programs such as HINARI and AGORA (the UN-initiated programs through which access is available for free or at very low charge to lesser-developed countries) has extended electronic journal availability to those who have never had access to print at all.

That is not to say that there are not readers who prefer print issues and will use those print issues in preference to electronic. But preference should be differentiated from actual lack of access.

Authors may well also be concerned about whether their articles will be as completely indexed and discoverable in electronic as in print. Again, this is a question that can be easily answered. There are now some abstracting and indexing services (notably Medline) that say they need assurance of acceptable digital archiving before they will include an e-only title in their coverage. This requires the publisher to provide assurance that archiving is taking place and may mean negotiation over the definition of a trusted archive. But this does not seem like an insurmountable hurdle. Where there are both print and electronic editions, traditional abstracting and indexing services increasingly use the electronic rather than the print as their source (for reasons of earlier availability and improved efficiency). In addition, search engineers such as Google and Scirus offer an entire additional and very powerful layer of access. Authors are only damaged by not being available electronically.

Authors also stand to benefit by being able to add multimedia objects, large data sets, and other interactive features to their articles. Against those benefits, there are other author concerns about the end of print. Those include:

- What can I do with my article? How can I use it, where can I post it and with whom can I share it (students, colleagues, others)? These issues are increasingly well-defined for authors and most authors have few or no complaints about what they can do with their own works.
- Will I still get reprints/offprints to distribute? If there are no print editions, it is unlikely that a publisher would provide traditional offprints. (One wonders how much these are used now anyway.)

However, authorization to use PDFs or other e-forwarding of articles, plus posting on institutional or personal websites, is increasingly rendering this a moot question.

- What about the integrity of the work? How can I be sure that my work will not be altered if it is only in e-form? This is an important question and one that relates to the need for several distributed preservation archives that can assure that the definitive version is, indeed, definitive. The converse of this is that e-only does offer easier opportunities to issue errata that travel with the work and have an audit trail to readily identify how an article has been changed.
- Will the end of print weaken the "brand" or identity of the journal and therefore my reflected prestige in publishing in that journal? Probably not but there is some need to re-enforce the journal name; more on that below on publishers' concerns.
- Will my citation rates change and will journal Impact Factors change? Citation rates should not be negatively affected–greater visibility means greater opportunity to be cited–and the tracking of citations is now much more widely done by a number of services beyond ISI. As for Impact Factors, this goes to journal reputation and branding and increasingly one should expect usage data to augment or otherwise be evaluated alongside of IFs.
- Finally, and of vital importance to younger scholars, will e-only journals be accepted on an equal basis for tenure or promotion decisions? While it is too early to say definitively, as major journals–particularly major society journals–make the switch to no printing of paper, the stature and evaluation criteria will have to follow along. This will likely be discipline-specific, and not be even across all fields.

Readers are often authors in another mode, but they clearly can be non-research practitioners (notably in medicine and engineering), students, and in some cases the general public. Their concerns mirror those of authors, looked at from the other side:

- Will I have reliable access?
- Will access be affordable?
- What am I allowed to do with the version I receive?
- Will the article be easily found and available for use again in two or 20 years if I want to reread it or review my research?
- How can I be sure I am looking at the official, definitive version?

Solving the concerns of authors will solve most of the concerns of readers as well. The critical core is ensuring easy, affordable, continuing access to a secure definitive version of the article.

PUBLISHERS

If librarians and administrators, authors and readers have questions that need to be answered if traditional journals are to close down print, publishers have the longest list of all. Clearly, there would be savings if there were no print at all for *all* of a publisher's titles:

* no need to maintain two production processes;
* no paper, printing, and binding expense;
* no postage or other shipping costs;
* no inventory to control or storage to pay for;
* no need to maintain separate order entry, invoicing, and customer service systems for print and electronic subscriptions; and
* greater simplicity in the sales process.

While most of these savings are real and quantifiable, the expectation must be that most, if not all, cost savings would have to be passed along to customers. So one could argue that publishers would be at best cost-neutral as to making the change and would only do so primarily to (1) satisfy customers and (2) simplify their own lives. However, publishers have to be careful, as there are pitfalls that could have a significant impact on their business, including revenue losses. Issues include:

* Are authors really satisfied with e-only or will they migrate to another publisher that is still maintaining print? Obviously manuscript flow is critically important for a journal, its editor and publisher. It is not just having enough papers but having the best papers from the best authors.
* What about current print-only subscribers? Will these subscribers convert to an electronic subscription if that is all that is available or will they simply cancel? While electronic-only subscriptions or print + electronic dominate, all traditional journals still have a significant number of print subscribers who have not yet embraced the electronic version. The reasons are many, e.g., preference for paper, poor electronic access, a single niche subscription within a large corporation. At some point publishers will reach the

breakeven point where it is no longer profitable to print, even though there are still print subscriptions, but until publishers reach that point, losing print-only subscriptions has adverse bottom line effects.

- Will the societies for whom we publish and their members accept e-only? Individuals often resist converting their favorite journal to e-reading and that journal is often their lead society title.
- What about medical journals and other journals with significant income from advertising? Will that source of revenue be transferable online? So far the medical advertising has not been easily moved, but that may be because the print alternative still exists. This needs serious research with both individual physicians as to their acceptance of e-versions and with pharmaceutical companies.
- Will we need to establish a print-on-demand service for those "requiring" bound print volumes? If so, this is not necessarily a bad thing, as it would be an additional revenue stream.
- As the electronic version becomes the definitive edition, what (if anything) needs to be added or changed to ensure that all information now in the print version is captured in the online version? This is a concern now in the print + electronic world and publishers have tried to address this. It is difficult to guarantee one-for-one matching when two editions exist. Advertising, as indicated, differs between paper and electronic. There may also be differences in the front matter–instructions to authors, listing of editorial boards, etc.–between paper and electronic. In many respects the elimination of print would be a benefit to all, as it would remove the concern about congruity–what is in the e-version is all there would be, period.
- Does the lack of a print cover and the absence of the physical handling of an issue weaken the brand identity and lead to changes not only in submission but in citation or other author, editor, or reader actions? Journal reputation–"branding"–is of importance whether one is dealing with a print or electronic-only journal. Clearly, electronic journals can establish excellent reputation quickly. Consider that the Public Library of Science Biology was born in 2003 as (primarily) an electronic journal and by mid 2005 it had already achieved an Impact Factor of 13.9 (per its website, www.plos.org). But PLoS Biology is also available in print, so even here the story is not unambiguous. One would think the risk is largely one of timing. If all journals from all publishers were to move together, the

relative position of one journal versus another would be less likely to change than if, as will happen, publishers will convert at different times. It may be that the journal name will become less significant in an all electronic world in any case, as more access is by searching, rather than Table of Content browsing. But that has been speculated upon for the past decade without a definitive conclusion.

- Will the timing of the end of print need to differ by discipline? Almost certainly that would be the ideal approach. What will most likely happen for the larger multi-disciplinary publishers is that there will be a toe-in-the-water experimental approach of first stopping the most obvious disciplines, those that appear to be least at risk of problems (physics comes to mind). Then, if that proceeds well, the decision will be made to do everything, as only then will savings be achieved for the publisher.

- Are there other ways to do this in stages? For example, stop doing print volume indices? This question came up at Elsevier in early 2006 and a consultation with our library advisory board members in North American and Europe brought a unanimous "yes, you can stop printing the indices," although some did ask for downloadable PDF versions for some journals. While it would be nice to stop creating the indices completely, a switch to downloadable PDF indices is a major step forward.

- How will the economic model change if there is no print (and, related, how will subscription agents be affected)? The economic model will likely change long before there is an elimination of the print version. First, the electronic version will become increasingly the definitive version, "flipping the model" from print to electronic as the base point. Second, for larger publishers there may be some options to approach all of their journals as a database, with pricing models that rely on metrics other than title-by-title subscription for pricing. These things will happen independently of the decision to end print.

This is a long list of publisher questions and concerns and many of these are solely publisher issues, affecting other stakeholders only to the degree that they inhibit publishers from making the change to eliminating print. However, just as with librarians, administrators, authors and readers, publishers share the fundamental concern about permanent future access to electronic journals. Publishers have a responsibility to both authors and the broader research community to ensure as well as they can that there is bullet-proof digital archiving of what they publish. This is not something that can be done in the same manner as with print, where publishers produced and delivered the issues and someone (or so one hoped) preserved them. At best, publishers saw their responsibility in the paper environment as the need to print on acid-free paper. In the digital world the responsibility is shared between publishers and libraries and each must play its role.

DIGITAL PRESERVATION OF JOURNALS AND ACCESS TO THOSE JOURNALS

The serious investigation of how to preserve electronic journals predates their widespread availability. Already in 1994, for example, RLG and the Commission on Preservation and Access (a predecessor of CLIR, the Commission on Library and Information Resources) formed a Task Force on Digital Archiving, whose report was issued in 1996 (a PDF version is available on the CLIR website at clir.org). Those of us on the Task Force struggled to get our hands around the issues that would have to be dealt with to put a successful digital archiving infrastructure in place, concluding that the legal and economic challenges may be greater than technical and organizational issues. Given where we are a decade later, we may have been more prescient than we thought at the time. One obvious example: the Google Library project in early 2006 is more about legality and money than the issues of how to technically create a digital archive (assuming this project has an archival mission–in itself a debatable assumption). And, to indicate how far some think we still have to go with digital archiving, at the first meeting of a new CLIR committee on preservation in February, 2006, when told of this presentation one preservationist reacted by noting "we've barely got preserving paper under control."

If digital archiving is far from resolved at this point and its critical importance is acknowledged if print is to stop, has nothing been accomplished over the past decade? I would argue that many advances have been made. These include:

- a recognition by most large publishers and some small that they have a responsibility for ensuring that archiving occurs in an acceptable manner;
- an acceptance on the part of libraries that archiving may require some level of partnering with publishers;

- the emergence of at least one national library (the Koninklijke Bibliotheek in The Netherlands) that has taken as part of its mission the preservation of e-journals on behalf of the international research community;
- the establishment of Portico, a non-profit organization also taking the dark archiving of e-journals as its mission;
- the launch of a two-year beta test for distributed dark archives within the LOCKSS framework (Controlled LOCKSS or CLOCKSS);
- a consideration on the part of many other national libraries about the possibility of establishing national archives of journals–something that provides some assurance to the international community as to the actual preservation of the electronic journals but little or no assurance as to access by anyone outside that country;
- the development of standards (such as OAIS) for archival use; and
- the beginnings of software systems that may become sufficiently robust to maintain large archives over time.

If these things are the good news, there are still important open questions to be resolved. These include:

- How will permanent digital archiving be funded over time? What is the role of publishers, individual libraries and national agencies in providing funding? The question of "who pays" has been at the heart of the archiving discussion from the beginning. The LOCKSS/CLOCKSS philosophy, for example, says that archiving must be done at the lowest possible marginal cost, in order to assure its sustainability across time, through lean budget years. This influences the technical design and approach to formal migration, for example. Some librarians have argued that publishers should bear all costs, yet it is publisher failure that is being insured against, so this has its logical limitations. Systems that rely on publishers for sole support are inherently suspect. Better is a system that involves all stakeholders.
- What constitutes a "trusted archive"? Who trusts whom and under what circumstances? Which nations are trusted by others?
- Is international e-journal archiving for the eventual use of the international research community something that is reasonable to expect of any individual university library?
- What access will there be to dark archives and by whom? What are the trigger events and when are they reversible? When the trigger events occur, will only those who have paid to build and maintain

the archive have access or will the whole research community benefit? And if the latter, is there a "free rider" problem?

- What specifically should be archived? Only the content or the look-and-feel, the links?
- What about version control? Journal articles are being made public in various phases of production, with the pressure to make them accessible (at least to subscribers) as soon as possible after acceptance. The articles will go through further copyediting and production stages and new versions will be posted, replacing the earlier version. What does this do to citation and version control? How will errors be corrected after "final publication" and how does that affect the archived version?
- Similarly, what of articles withdrawn from online services? It is never the desire of the editor or publisher that a published article (or an "article in press") be withdrawn, but in some instances it is unavoidable. Continuing to make the article available to the public when it may, for example, have information that is so inaccurate that it would result in medical harm or where it has been found to be fraudulent in other ways is not acceptable. Is the article removed from the archive also? Is it "sequestered"–no longer shown by the archive but still there, should it need to be retrieved for some reason in the future and, in any case, to maintain a complete record?
- What assurances are there that the archive will be physically accessible over time (as data storage formats change) and the data integrity maintained? These are the critical technology issues that have been debated over and over for the last fifteen years but there still is no absolute reassurance that either migration or emulation will be sustainable. At this point we proceed on the basis of testing and faith.

IN CONCLUSION

So, what to conclude from these infrequently asked questions–questions that must be answered satisfactorily if publishers are to stop the printing of journals. Clearly all stakeholders–librarians, institutional administrators, authors and readers–have legitimate issues to be addressed. And publishers have their own questions, some of which could have significant effect on their business models. Archiving is clearly the sine qua non for all. If we want to end print, we must have bullet-proof digital archiving of electronic journals. We are making progress, but there are many, many issues still to be settled.

Does that mean we should just put this question–when can we end print–back on the shelf for another decade? As one librarian said recently, the publisher will know when to stop when everyone stops buying print, simple as that. I don't think it is that simple, although it does indicate the need to at least calculate at which point the costs of printing outweigh the income from the sale of the print copies. If ending print is truly an important change that librarians and their administrators want, then we will have to work together to make it happen. Are the questions raised above the right ones? What is missing? How do we get answers? Most importantly, how do we get that "bullet-proof" digital archiving? Perhaps working together–librarians, scholars, and publishers–as partners in exploring the concerns, we can make progress. There could be a high level of risk for publishers, but we won't advance without taking risk.

doi:10.1300/J111v46n02_09

Index

Page numbers followed by f indicate figures; those marked with t indicate tables.

ABC-CLIO, 63
Accessibility Institute, 7
Acock Associates, 36
Age of Empires, Civilization, or Rome: Total War, 23
AGORA, 124
American Antiquarian Society, 85
American Civil War, 19
American Library Association
    Mid-Winter meeting, 6
Andrew W. Mellon Foundation, 76
AnthroSource for Anthropology, 63
Architecture Library, 28,30f
Archiving, in JSTOR, 64-67,65f,66f
Area Studies Microform Projects, 103
Article Express, 45
Association of Research Libraries, 40
Atkinson, R., 110,111
Author(s), end of print journals views
    of, 123-126

Bacon, F., 88
Baidu, 84
Behavior(s), information-seeking,
    evolving, impact on research
    libraries, case study of, 3-16.
    See also Information-seeking
    behaviors, evolving, impact
    on research libraries, case
    study of
Behavioral issues, in case study of
    evolving information-seeking

behaviors impact on research
    libraries, 14-16
Bennet, S., 34,45-46
Benson, N.L., 5
Berkeley University, 102
Billings, H., 5
Blooker Prize, 20
"Blooks," 20
Book(s), promoting of, through digital,
    visual displays, 23-24
Bowen, W.G., 57,58
Bradlee, B., 80
Branin, J.J., 27
British Library, 81
Brookings Institution, 83
Buckland, M.K., 87

Cambridge Scientific Abstracts, 63
Carlton, D., 5
Carnegie, 84
Caste mentalities, in cooperative
    conundrum in digital age,
    115-117
Center for Research Libraries,
    85,103,117
Cheshire system interface, 97,98f
Child, J., 20
Civil War, 80
CLIR. *See* Commission on Library and
    Information Resources
    (CLIR)

Milton Keynes UK
Ingram Content Group UK Ltd.
UKHW031151141024
449569UK00024B/875